The Case for a
Maximum Wage

The Case For series

Sam Pizzigati, *The Case for a Maximum Wage*

Sam Pizzigati

The Case for a Maximum Wage

polity

The right of Sam Pizzigati to be identified as Author of this Work has been asserted in accordance with the UK Copyright, Designs and Patents Act 1988.

First published in 2018 by Polity Press

Polity Press
65 Bridge Street
Cambridge CB2 1UR, UK

Polity Press
101 Station Landing
Suite 300
Medford, MA 02155, USA

ISBN-13: 978-1-5095-2491-4
ISBN-13: 978-1-5095-2492-1 (pb)

A catalogue record for this book is available from the British Library.

Library of Congress Cataloging-in-Publication Data

Names: Pizzigati, Sam, author.
Title: The case for a maximum wage / Sam Pizzigati.
Description: Cambridge, UK ; Medford, MA : Polity Press, 2018. | Series: The case for | Includes bibliographical references and index.
Identifiers: LCCN 2017048524 (print) | LCCN 2017050835 (ebook) | ISBN 9781509524952 (Epub) | ISBN 9781509524914 (hardback) | ISBN 9781509524921
 (pbk.)
Subjects: LCSH: Wages--Government policy--United States. | Rich people--Government policy--United States. | Equality--United States.
Classification: LCC HD4975 (ebook) | LCC HD4975 .P27 2018 (print) | DDC 331.2/3--dc23
LC record available at https://lccn.loc.gov/2017048524

Typeset in 11 on 15 Sabon by Servis Filmsetting Ltd, Stockport, Cheshire
Printed and bound in the United Kingdom by Clays Ltd, St Ives PLC

For further information on Polity, visit our website:politybooks.com

Contents

For Pablo, Chaly, and Tomás

Acknowledgments

I've been writing about inequality – and the notion of a "maximum wage" – for almost three decades now. I can't seem to stop. That may be because the societies I know best keep getting more unequal. Or maybe I just enjoy hanging out with egalitarians, most notably my collaborators on Inequality.org.

My thanks to everyone whose ideas and encouragement have shaped this slender volume. A special appreciation to New York labor activist Jeff Vogel and Canadian researcher Jacob David Poulin-Litvak, two indefatigables on all things maximum wage related.

These chapters also owe much of the value they may have to the patient scrutiny of ace readers Nancy Leibold and Carl Luty. My deepest thanks as well to my eminently thoughtful editors at Polity, George Owers and Justin Dyer. And my deepest

Acknowledgments

gratitude, as always, goes to Karabelle. She may not have lived long enough to peruse these pages, but her wisdom and compassion, after nearly a half-century together, remain my rock.

Sam Pizzigati
October 2017

Introduction

Moderation in All Things, Even Income

Most of us shy away from excess. Everything works better, we understand, in moderation. Too much of anything, even essentials for our health and humanity, does us no good. Too much food can leave us dangerously obese. Too much strenuous exercise can break down our bodies. Even too much love can become suffocatingly obsessive.

Excess creates messes. Societies grasp this reality almost instinctively – and set limits to keep excess at bay. We limit how fast motorists can drive. We limit how much waste factory owners can dump in our rivers. We limit how much noise our neighbors can make.

But we don't set limits on everything. We do not limit personal income. We have no "speed limit" on how rapidly the rich can become richer. And they have become richer. Phenomenally richer.

1

Introduction

Many of our most compelling numbers on global fortunes come from the annual wealth reports the Credit Suisse Research Institute began publishing in 2010. Midway through 2017, Credit Suisse calculates, the world's wealthiest 1 percent held 50.1 percent of global wealth, more than the rest of the world combined.

Those who hold truly grand fortunes – over $50 million in net worth – make up just a tiny fraction of the wealthy who can claim global top 1 percent status.[1] Credit Suisse counts over 148,000 of these "ultra-high net worth" fortunes, with about half in the United States.

The richest of the ultra rich, the world's billionaires, now total over 2,000. The least of these billionaires now hold 279,000 times more personal wealth than our planet's typical adult.

The activist charity Oxfam has translated the Credit Suisse numbers into some memorable images. In 2009, the group points out, the world's 380 richest billionaires – a cohort small enough to fit into a jumbo jetliner – held as much wealth as humanity's poorest half. By 2017, the combined fortunes of just 42 billionaires could offset the entire net worth of the 3.7 billion people who make up the world's bottom half.[2] These eight could ride comfortably in a standard-sized city-bus.

Introduction

This top-heavy distribution of the world's treasure, some maintain, rates as no big deal. Think of all the entertainment value the super rich create, they quip. How could we live without the Instagrams of young wealthy heirs "flaunting their Rolexes, Maybachs and pet lions"?[3] One recent British TV series took viewers "behind the scenes at a luxury hotel to reveal the extravagant and ridiculous requests of the rich and famous."[4] In one episode, a guest checks in with 200 pieces of luggage, a bride insists on an elephant for her wedding party, and a gentleman of means wants his socks pressed. We're expected to giggle at their vanities.

Most of the world, fortunately, sees vast gaps in income and wealth as no laughing matter. Inequality has become, as Barack Obama observed early in his second term, the "defining challenge of our time."[5]

"A world in which 1 percent of humanity controls as much wealth as the other 99 percent," Obama added in a United Nations address, "will never be stable."[6]

Leading global figures have echoed those sentiments. Pope Francis has labeled inequality "the root of social evil." Nobel Peace Prize laureate Muhammad Yunus, the celebrated founder of the microfinance movement, has described the concentration of the world's wealth as a "ticking time bomb."[7] In 2014, a survey of over 1,700 global movers and shakers set to attend the annual World Economic Forum in Davos identified "deepening income inequality" as the world's most pressing issue.[8]

People worldwide, the Washington, DC-based Pew Research Center has found, share a similar perspective.[9] Pew surveyed 44 nations in 2015. Majorities in all 44 called the gap between rich and poor "a big problem facing their countries."

All these anxieties about our economic divides rest upon a veritable explosion of research into inequality's impact on our daily lives and long-term prospects. Over the last quarter-century, the International Social Science Council reports, the number of studies on inequality-related concerns has increased "five-fold."[10]

Much of this new research involves the United States, the world's most unequal developed nation. In the United States, as elsewhere, inequality endangers almost everything we hold dear. Divorce rates run the highest in American counties where inequality has increased the fastest. US states with income highly concentrated at the economic summit have more carbon emissions and weaker environmental protections. Highly unequal states also have higher incidences of hate crimes.[11] Just plain civility suffers, too, in less equal jurisdictions. People in America's most unequal states, notes University of Melbourne psychologist Nick Haslam, "score relatively low on agreeableness" and show more willingness "to engage in immoral behaviour."[12]

Researchers have found stark differences between more and less unequal jurisdictions at the national level as well. In 2009, the British social scientists Richard Wilkinson and Kate Pickett brought these differences to global attention with their landmark book, *The Spirit Level: Why Greater Equality Makes Us Stronger*, since published in some two dozen foreign editions. People in more unequal developed nations, *The Spirit Level* revealed, can be anywhere from two to ten times more likely than people in more equal nations to be obese or get murdered, to mistrust others or have a pregnant teen daughter, to become a drug addict or end up in prison.

Earlier work by Wilkinson and Pickett had focused attention on what may be inequality's most dramatic impact: People in more equal nations live significantly longer than people in less equal nations. The distinctly unequal United States ranks close to the developed world basement on life expectancy – despite spending on health care *almost triple* the developed world per capita average.[13] If current trends continue, the medical journal *Lancet* reported in 2017, American lifespans – once among the world's longest – will by 2030 stretch no longer than lifespans in Mexico, a far less prosperous nation.[14]

News reports typically blame America's shockingly low life-expectancy rates on a lack of access to affordable health care or poverty or poor personal habits. But epidemiologists – scientists who study health outcomes – point out that the United States ranked as one of the world's healthiest nations in the 1950s, a time when ample numbers of Americans smoked heavily, ate a diet that would horrify any twenty-first-century nutritionist, and hardly ever exercised. Poor Americans, then as now, had chronic problems accessing health care. And poverty, epidemiologists add, can't explain why fully insured middle-income Americans today live shorter, less healthy lives than middle-income people in other rich nations.

What can explain these shorter, less healthy lives? Epidemiologists cite what they call "the social determinants of health." The more inequality in a society, the more stress. Chronic stress, over time, wears down our immune systems and leaves us more vulnerable to disease. This same stress drives people to seek relief in unhealthy habits. They may do drugs or smoke – or eat more "comfort foods" packed with sugar and fat.

Inequality has an equally potent impact on health-related public policy.

Much of our adult health, University of Washington epidemiologist Stephen Bezruchka explains, gets programmed into us at an early age.[15] Given this reality, guaranteeing every child adequate support in the early years ought to be *the* top priority for any society committed to better health for all. But more unequal nations do precious little of this guaranteeing. They regularly appear at the bottom of global rankings for child well-being.[16]

Why do more unequal nations so consistently shortchange children? Their behavior at first glance seems inexplicable. No politicians in modern democracies ever campaign *against* kids. So why doesn't public policy in unequal nations adequately *support* kids? The answer may well lie in the most classic of inequality critiques: Intense concentrations of wealth, political thinkers have long argued, undermine democratic governance. Among these thinkers: the Americans who founded the world's first modern republic in 1776.

"The Founders understood full well that if severe economic inequality emerged," writes Vanderbilt

University legal scholar Ganesh Sitaraman, "their democratic experiment would collapse."[17]

In the contemporary United States, severe economic inequality *has* emerged, and that emergence has political scientists studying whether the nation even still rates the democracy label. Northwestern University's Benjamin Page and Princeton's Martin Gilens have crunched 20 years of data – on nearly 1,800 policy issues – to see how well contemporary American politics "responds to the wishes of the average citizen."[18]

What do the data show?

"If you observe the United States right now, you discover that the average citizen has no detectable influence on policy," notes Page. "That's not much of a democracy."

The deeply unequal Philippines also rates as not much of a democracy, and local business leaders like Henry Schumacher of the Filipino European Chamber of Commerce see inequality as the culprit: "Inequality breeds corruption and leads to a dependency of the poor on their political leaders."[19] Corruption, in turn, aggravates inequality: Only the well-off can afford to bribe. An unholy trinity – inequality, corruption, and mistrust – creates a "vicious circle" almost impossible to bust.

In unequal nations, agrees a 2016 International

Monetary Fund analysis, people simply trust others less.[20] Its authors, Alexander Hijzen and Eric Gould, posit that this may be one reason why inequality undercuts economic growth and development. Over recent years, the world's three prime global economic institutions – the IMF, the World Bank, and the OECD, a government-funded economic think tank for the developed world – have all chimed in with research that directly ties inequality to economic dysfunction.

A generation ago, ironically, mainstream economists believed that greater *equality* fostered dysfunction. Any attempts to restrain incomes at the top, this mainstream held, would reduce incentives to save and invest and throttle the economic growth necessary to "lift all boats." But that mainstream has reversed course and now sees inequality as more likely to sink boats than lift them.[21] Rising income inequality, IMF managing director Christine Lagarde warned in 2014, is casting a "dark shadow" across the global economy.[22] Reversing inequality's "long-run rise," the OECD noted the same year, "would not only make societies less unfair, but also richer."[23]

Economists and epidemiologists, psychologists and political scientists: Researchers from multiple disciplines have detailed the high price we pay when we tolerate intense maldistributions of income and wealth. If we want a world more welcoming to the best humanity can be, the social science consensus holds, we need to narrow the gaps that divide us.

But how? Here we have no clear consensus. We do have options. Societies can narrow the gaps in income that distance our most and least affluent in three basic ways. We can level up incomes at the bottom of our economic order. We can level down incomes at the top. Or we can do both.

Those who sit atop our economic order – and those who seek their favor – typically do their best to confine us to the first of these options. To narrow our economic divides, friends of grand fortune advise, we need to work at lifting up the bottom. Fighting inequality, they maintain, need only involve attacking poverty, nothing more.

Raising a society's bottom-most incomes can certainly narrow a gap between rich and poor. But that gap can also widen if incomes at the top rise more rapidly than incomes at the bottom. China has witnessed this exact phenomenon over recent decades. Between 1978 and 2015, incomes for China's poorest 50 percent saw a real increase of 401 percent. In those same years, however, incomes for China's top 1 percent soared over four times faster, by 1,898 percent.[24] China has become considerably *more* unequal.

Still, tens of millions of Chinese families have gained greater economic security over the past four decades, and those who see inequality as purely a problem of *poverty* find China's experience encouraging. We need not fret about how well the rich may be doing, they argue, if the poor are doing better, too. Some take this stance a step further. Worrying about the rich, they maintain, only serves to distract us from the far more important task of lifting up the poor. Why obsess over the luxury in our penthouses, as former Bill Clinton aide Laura D'Andrea Tyson once asked, when people are living in rat-infested basements?[25]

We should be focusing on helping society's poorest, not hammering on the richest, adds Princeton economist Alan Blinder, a frequent advisor to Democratic Party presidential hopefuls. For the poor, Blinder believes, "the fantastic earnings of people that make $100 million a year are completely irrelevant."[26]

In its late 1990s heyday, the leadership of the UK Labour Party under Tony Blair held that increases in the grand fortunes of the rich can even speed the demise of dire poverty. The richer the rich become, the argument went, the more they can shell out at tax time to fund social programs for the poor. We are "intensely relaxed about people getting filthy rich," as Blair cabinet heavyweight Peter Mandelson famously put the matter in 1998, "as long as they pay their taxes."

But a decade and a half later, in an interview with the BBC, Mandelson would somewhat change his tune. "I don't think I would say that now," he acknowledged.[27] Mandelson's second thoughts shouldn't surprise us. Societies that "relax" on the rich don't get, in return, economies that benefit everyone. They get economies that benefit the rich – at everyone else's expense.

This dynamic has played out most dramatically in the United States. America's political elites, Republicans and Democrats alike, have been intensely relaxing on the rich ever since the late 1970s. They have reduced the taxes the rich pay and deregulated the businesses the rich run. The result? Since 1978, the poorest 50 percent of Americans have actually seen their real incomes shrink, by 1 percent. By contrast, America's most affluent 1 percent, over that same span, have seen their real incomes nearly triple.[28]

A recent World Bank report finds similar trends on the international front. Stagnation below, windfalls above. "Without significant shifts in within-country inequalities," the report concludes, the World Bank's current core goal – the elimination of extreme poverty by 2030 – "cannot be achieved."[29]

In China, meanwhile, the days of rapidly rising incomes – at the economic base – have come and gone. Over the last decade, real wages in the pace-setting city of Hong Kong have increased a grand total of 3 percent.[30] The poorest of Hong Kong's poor are now living in wire-mesh boxes stacked on top of apartment-house roofs. The boxes typically run six feet long and three feet wide. Locals call their occupants "caged dogs."[31]

China has not conquered poverty. No nation has. But some nations have dealt poverty much more than glancing blows. These more successful societies all value a more equitable distribution of the wealth their people create. They tax their rich. They regulate their economies. They underwrite public services that all their people can access. They endeavor to both level up and level down. They understand that any offensive against inequality that winks at grand fortune will sputter and stall long before society's poorest realize any lasting relief.

Any offensive against inequality that *only* focuses on the rich will, to be sure, also come up short. No decent society can tolerate destitution. But decency comes easiest when societies do their best to limit grand concentrations of private wealth. The more wealth the wealthy amass, the more political power the wealthy gain. The greater their power, the more that their concerns – and their concerns alone – drive what government does and does not do.

Governments the rich dominate do good by the rich. They cut their taxes. They address their aggravations. They help them become richer. Amid this do-gooding for the rich, the needs of middle-income households go ignored. Middle-class people in these households look above their economic station and see the rich and their tax avoidance. They look below and see the poor and their "handouts." They start seething. Any empathy they may feel for those less fortunate drains away, as does their support for the programs that bring decency to those of modest means or no means at all.

Peter Edelman, a former US Department of Health and Human Services assistant secretary and one of America's most respected poverty-fighters, has watched this process play out.[32]

"I used to believe," Edelman reflects, "that the debate over wealth distribution should be conducted separately from the poverty debate, in order to minimize the attacks on antipoverty advocates

14

for engaging in 'class warfare.' But now we literally cannot afford to separate the two issues."

The "economic and political power of those at the top," Edelman continues, is "making it virtually impossible to find the resources to do more at the bottom."

Campaigners for social justice over a century ago, during our modern world's first Gilded Age, came to the same conclusion. Level up *and* level down, they urged. Social reformer Joseph Pulitzer, the foremost newspaper publisher of his day, exhorted America in 1907 to "always oppose privileged classes" and "never be afraid to attack wrong, whether by predatory plutocracy or predatory poverty."

How should we go about attacking these twin predators? We have wide global agreement on the "predatory poverty" side. Most nations now understand that decency demands a minimum wage, an income floor that guarantees everyone who works – at least in theory – enough income to escape poverty and enjoy a modicum of economic security and dignity. In practice, contemporary minimum wages almost everywhere fall short of that noble goal. Many millions of people worldwide work full-time – and more – at minimum-wage jobs and still live in poverty.

But what if we applied a "maximum wage" to

our staggeringly unequal economic orders? What if each of our societies set a ceiling on the annual income any one individual could pocket – and linked this maximum to an existing wage minimum? Could this coupling set us on a more effective and lasting egalitarian course?

These pages will argue that linking minimums to newly created maximums would offer us our best hope yet at creating societies that work for all who live within them. In a world of only minimums, the pressure – from the powerful – to keep those minimums low and inadequate will always be unrelenting. The lower the minimum wage, the higher the potential reward for those who employ minimum-wage workers.

In a world of minimums *and* maximums, this powerful incentive to exploit society's weakest and most vulnerable would erode and eventually evaporate. In any nation that linked minimum to maximum, society's richest would be able to increase their own personal income only if the incomes of society's poorest increased first. In such a society, the rich would have a vested personal interest in enhancing the well-being of the poor. The exploiters would have cause to appreciate the value of social solidarity.

This vision of a more equitable tomorrow does,

of course, invite skeptical questions at every turn. Just how, for instance, would we define a "maximum wage"? Today's richest typically receive only a portion of their annual incomes from their "wages," the paychecks they draw. A "maximum wage" narrowly defined as a cap on just paycheck income would leave other income streams – rents, royalties, and returns from investments – intact and unchecked. And even if we do define our "maximum wage" more expansively, what about asset inequality? How could a maximum wage – a cap on *income* – speak to our already existing and massive inequalities of *wealth*? A few billionaires currently hold more wealth than half of humanity. In a world of wealth – and power – so unequally divided, how could a maximum wage ever become more than an idle political daydream?

Good questions. Our pages ahead have answers.

1

Defining Excess

Where does excess – in income – begin? At what point should society step in and say to any one individual that you simply make too much? Does too much begin at $1 million a year? Or £250,000? Or ¥500,000?

Any specific cap on monetary income, let's acknowledge at the outset, would have to be somewhat arbitrary. In the natural world, numbers that divide one state from another can be specific and unassailable. Water boils at 100 degrees centigrade. Water freezes at zero. In human social relations, by contrast, absolute numerical certainty will forever remain beyond our reach. Any limits we set in human affairs will always be at least a little bit capricious.

Take speed limits. Many nations limit speeds on major thoroughfares to no more than 110 kilometers per hour. But if we shifted that limit to 108 or 111, traffic would move along just as safely. None of us would consider this imprecision a reason to go without limits on how fast we drive. Any specific speed limit, we understand, will always reflect a judgment call. We humans can make good judgments. We can make poor judgments. Perfect judgments? Those we cannot make.

Minimum wage levels reflect our imperfections. The United States now has metropolitan areas where employers in one political jurisdiction must by law pay their workers at least $15 per hour while employers right next door in adjoining jurisdictions can legally get by paying a mere $7.25. Some public officials have clearly made a poor judgment. Workers in both the $15 and $7.25 jurisdictions have similar basic needs. The minimum required to live in decency simply cannot be twice as high in one jurisdiction as another.

In situations like these, those of us who care about fairness do not throw up our hands in frustration – or rail against the foolishness of trying to set a minimum wage. We instead commit ourselves to mending our inadequate minimums. We press public officials to make better judgments.

Similar dynamics would be at play with any future maximum wage. Specific maximum set-points would surely evolve over time, just as minimum wage levels have evolved. In the United States, employers had to pay only 25 cents an hour to meet the standard that the first national minimum wage set in 1938. The national minimum since then has increased, after adjusting for inflation, by two-thirds.

Let's also acknowledge another basic imprecision in these musings on maximums. Our label of choice for the policy outcome we seek, a "maximum wage," does not quite connote all that we need our label to express. We seek ultimately a cap on personal *income*. But setting a cap on *wages* – the compensation individuals receive in exchange for their labor – will not necessarily limit *income* because paychecks make up only one element of income, especially for our richest. An income cap that limits only compensation would leave our overall economic divides still unconscionably wide – and dangerous. We need more than a cap on wages.

So why aren't egalitarians talking about a "maximum income"? The "maximum wage" label simply makes more sense to more people. Most of us already understand why we need *minimum* wages. A "maximum wage" phrasing builds on this understanding, the prime reason why advocates for capping income so commonly use it.

We could, to be sure, choose to define a maximum wage more literally. Laws that establish minimum wages require employers to pay workers at least a set specific sum. A law establishing a maximum wage could do the exact reverse and explicitly prohibit employers from paying anyone more than a set specific sum.

This approach has never attracted much interest among egalitarians. Most "maximum wage" proposals over the years have instead involved taxing away all income over a particular point. One of the earliest of these proposals came from the German-born philosopher Felix Adler. In 1880, Adler proposed a steeply graduated income tax, with a 100 percent top rate at the point "when a certain high and abundant sum has been reached, amply sufficient for all the comforts and true refinements of life." This 100 percent top rate, Adler explained to a packed Gilded Age lecture hall in New York City, would leave any wealthy man with "all that he can *truly* use for the humane purposes of life" and tax away "only that which is to him merely a means of pomp and pride and power."

Coverage in the *New York Times* gave Adler's call for an income maximum some significant circulation,[1] but the notion of a maximum wage wouldn't take specific legislative shape in the United States until World War I, when progressives demanded a 100 percent tax on all income over $100,000 to more equitably finance the war effort. Their energetic efforts would totally alter the tenor of America's political discourse on taxes. The nation's top tax rate on income over $1 million, just 7 percent in 1914, would soar to 77 percent in 1918.

That top rate would sink back down to 25 percent in the 1920s, in the wake of the "Red Scare" that hammered the progressive movement right after World War I. But egalitarians would regain the political momentum during the Great Depression in the 1930s, and then a world war would once again shake up the tax structure. In 1942, just months after Pearl Harbor, President Franklin D. Roosevelt called for a 100 percent tax on individual income over $25,000, the equivalent of about $375,000 today. Lawmakers in Congress didn't give FDR his 100 percent top rate. But they did before the war's end hike the top tax rate on income over $200,000 to a record 94 percent.

America's top tax rate would hover around 90 percent for the next 20 years, a span that would witness the emergence of the first mass middle class in world history. By 1960, the clear majority of Americans, after paying for the basics of food and shelter, had disposable income. That had never happened before, in any modern nation. But the United States would not remain exceptional for long. In the decades after World War II, nations throughout the developed world taxed the rich stiffly and grew the middle class quickly.

Most of the developed world, in these post-war years, became significantly more equal. Back in 1928, the year before the Great Depression began, America's top 1 percent had raked in nearly a quarter of the nation's income, the bottom 90 percent only half. By 1970, the top 1 percent share had dropped below a tenth of the nation's income total, and the share going to America's bottom 90 percent had jumped to over two-thirds.[2]

European nations witnessed similar distributional shifts over the same period.[3] In the United Kingdom, the top 1 percent's share of national income dipped from nearly 20 to just over 5 percent, in France from over 23 to under 9 percent. In Sweden, the top 1 percent income share plummeted from over 28 to under 4 percent.

This mid-twentieth-century egalitarian success raises an obvious political question for those of us who advocate capping, not just robustly taxing, income at society's summit. Why bother struggling for an outright lid on income – a daunting political task in even the most favorable of circumstances –

when history shows that an income tax with steeply graduated tax rates can usher in substantially higher levels of economic equality?

In fact, we have good cause for not simply seeking to restore the steeply graduated progressive tax rates of the mid-twentieth century. Those steep tax rates could not be sustained. In the United States, they lasted a generation, only slightly longer in other developed nations.

Why did high tax rates on high incomes disappear? The rich did them in.

In the United States, the mid-twentieth-century rich longed for the comfortable world that "confiscatory" tax rates had upended. America's wealthiest felt "battered by the income tax," as *Fortune*, America's leading business magazine, reported in 1955. Some top corporate executives, the influential magazine related, "may cough up" to Uncle Sam "as much as 75 per cent" of their total incomes. Back in 1930, *Fortune* wistfully noted, the high-salaried executive "arrived at his office in his chauffeur-driven Pierce-Arrow." His 1955 counterparts, by contrast, were driving themselves "through the morning chaos." Early twentieth-century private yachts early had stretched over 300 feet long. In the America of the 1950s, *Fortune* lamented, 75 feet had come to seem "a lot of yacht."[4]

But the wealthy did more than grouse against America's mid-century tax progressivism. They connived to subvert the federal tax code at every opportunity. They schemed to puncture the code with new loopholes. They bankrolled candidates who pledged to protect the precious loopholes – like the enormously lucrative oil depletion allowance – that had somehow survived Franklin Roosevelt's New Deal tax offensive. Above all else, wealthy Americans pressed for lower tax rates on income in the top tax brackets. They considered high tax rates a direct personal affront and felt viscerally invested in the drive to cut these rates back. Every point the rich could manage to shave off the nation's top tax rate would, they fervently believed, speed chauffeurs and long, lush yachts back into their lives.

The wealthy, in other words, had an intense personal stake in lowering top-bracket tax rates, and this intense stake gave the twentieth-century political debate over tax rates a basic – and ongoing – asymmetry. The aggrieved rich could see an immediate personal payoff from lower top rates. For everyone else, that immediacy just didn't kick in. The real and significant benefits average Americans were gaining from high taxes on high incomes were playing out too subtly to see.

High tax rates on high incomes, for instance, gave

top corporate executives less incentive to exploit workers and shortchange consumers. Why make the effort to squeeze still another dollar of profit out of ordinary-income people when the personal gains that squeezing might bring would face a tax rate of over 90 percent?

This sort of benefit from significantly taxing the rich went largely unappreciated. Ordinary-income people felt no compelling personal need to keep top tax rates high. That left the rich with motive and opportunity to pull off the perfect class-war crime.

In the United States, the top income-bracket tax rate fell from 91 percent in 1963 to 70 percent in 1965 to 50 percent in 1982 to 28 percent in 1988, before bouncing around and ending up, at the close of the Obama years, at 39.6 percent. In 2017, even with two additional special taxes put in place to help finance the Obama health care reform, America's richest were on average paying federal income taxes at less than half the rate their wealthy forebears paid in the mid-twentieth century.

Tax rates in the United Kingdom underwent a similar downward spiral. The top British tax rate – 97.5 percent at the end of World War II – had spiraled down to 40 percent by the late 1980s. The French top rate, 90 percent on the eve of World War II, was hovering at 65 percent in 1983 and then dropped to 40 percent in 2007. In New Zealand, the top rate fell by half in the 1980s, from 66 to 33 percent. Most everywhere in the developed world, the same trajectory held. Top rates fell. They could not be sustained, and that failure may well be built into the DNA of the progressive income tax as traditionally structured. The rich simply have much more of a direct personal stake in sabotaging high taxes on high incomes than the rest of us have in keeping those taxes whole.

Could that change? Could we somehow transform the traditional progressive income tax and give those of modest means a more direct personal stake in the taxes paid by people of excessively ample means? Could we, in the same transformation, give the rich an incentive for *not* obsessively seeking to obliterate tax progressivism? We certainly could – if we began linking incomes at the top of our economic order to incomes far below.

Some analysts are making this connection. One proposal along this line, from Yale law professor Ian Ayres and University of California economist Aaron Edlin, would have US tax collectors annually compute the income equal to 36 times the nation's median household income. If the average taxpayer in the top 1 percent makes more than this 36-times figure, this proposal would have the government put in place a special annual tax rate that reduces average 1-percenter incomes to the 36-times level.[5]

A far simpler and much bolder approach – and the approach that these pages advocate – would be to set a new income maximum as a multiple of the existing minimum wage. Any income above that multiple would face a tax set at 100 percent.

How would this work? Let's use the United States for our example. A worker laboring at the federal minimum wage currently earns $7.25 an hour, a rate that would return $15,080 for a standard 40-hour week over the course of an entire year. This $15,080 would become the base for calculating the income maximum. If society set that maximum at 100 times the minimum wage, that maximum would be $1,508,000. Any income above that $1,508,000 would face a 100 percent federal tax rate.

This maximum would apply to all income an individual taxpayer reports, whatever the source. And the maximum for a couple filing a joint tax return would be twice that $1,508,000, or $3,016,000.

A "maximum wage" set in this fashion would immediately intertwine the economic fates of society's poorest and society's most privileged. Those with too much "pomp and pride and power," to use Felix Adler's classic nineteenth-century formulation, would suddenly have a substantial incentive to care deeply about the well-being of those they over-shadow economically. Society's wealthiest would only be able to increase their own after-tax incomes if those who toil in the darkest shadows – minimum-wage workers – saw their incomes increase first.

These toilers would soon find themselves basking in society's spotlight. Improving their well-being would become the central focus of any society that linked top incomes to incomes at the economic base. Minimum-wage workers would strive to keep this linkage in place. And so would workers making just above the minimum wage. The "ripple effect" of a higher minimum wage would raise their pay-checks, too – and help build a sizeable constituency of working people personally committed to the preservation of any multiple-based maximum. The political asymmetry that doomed high tax rates on high incomes in the twentieth century would be no more. A multiple maximum would be sustainable.

But what should the ideal multiple be? The 100 times of our example above? Twice that? Half that? The creative imaging of the late Danish economist Jan Pen suggests an even smaller multiple.

In a classic 1971 book, Pen asks us to visualize Britain's distribution of income as an hour-long parade, with income earners marching in income order, from lowest to highest.[6] Pen's parade has a special touch. Each marcher's height corresponds to each marcher's income. Average income earners have average heights. Marchers making half a society's average income stand only half average height. Marchers making double the average stretch up twice as tall as that average.

Pen's hour-long parade begins. The poorest of the poor walk by us first, all tinier than any adult human has ever been. In short order, the working poor walk past us, all small of stature, but now recognizably human. The marchers slowly grow taller, to average height and then to seven feet. Finally, in the parade's closing moments, the marchers begin to lose all human scale. Their heights suddenly start soaring. Fifty feet tall, one hundred feet, one *mile* high – much too high to have any human interaction with any other marchers.

Researchers have over the years applied the "Pen parade" framing to many different modern societies. They find the same basic pattern that Pen's initial parade revealed: a slow, steady, incremental increase in the height of the marchers, then a sudden surge upwards. Within that first phase, real human interactions can abound. Everyone who marches before the parade surge, as the British economist Henry Phelps Brown once noted, "rubs elbows with others who are a little better or worse off."[7] After the surge, the marchers become parading giants who can rub shoulders with only their fellow rich.

"Pen parades" do vary by individual society. In more equal nations, the marchers at the end do not soar quite so high. But in all developed modern societies, the soaring will begin at a similar point, and that point seems to come when incomes at the back end of the parade begin exceeding about 10 times the incomes of the first recognizably human-sized marchers.[8] Societies that blow past this 10-to-1 ratio have entered the danger zone, a place where meaningful human contact between the rich and everyone else becomes ever more difficult and ever less likely.

The giants of our "Pen parades" cannot possibly see the joy or the pain on the faces of marchers who stand just three or six or even a dozen feet tall. If we want our rich and the rest of society near enough economically to witness and feel their shared humanity, we cannot let these giants roam. We would instead avoid that danger zone that Pen's parade reveals. We would keep after-tax incomes at our economic summit no more than 10 times the minimum incomes at society's base.

Could entire modern societies ever fit themselves into the confines of a 10-to-1 income ratio between top and bottom? Today, in most all the world's nations, that hardly seems possible. Incomes have become so unequally distributed that visualizing a top-to-bottom ratio of even 100-to-1 has become deflatingly difficult. In 2015, for instance, America's wealthiest needed to collect at least $11.3 million in income to enter the ranks of the nation's most affluent 0.01 percent.[9] The affluents in this top 0.01 percent averaged $31.6 million in income, nearly *2,100 times* the annual income of an American working full-time at a minimum-wage job.

Let's make this math a little more vivid: a minimum-wage worker in the United States would have to work two entire *millennia* to match a single year's haul of America's top 0.01 percenters.

So, given these millennia-wide multiples, how could we proceed to meet our daunting egalitarian task in hand? What could we do to ease our societies toward an income cap, a "maximum wage" realized via a 100 percent levy on income above and beyond a set multiple of our income minimums?

What could we do? We could narrow our initial focus, from societies writ large to a pivotal single element within our societies: the corporate enterprise. These enterprises largely determine who gets what in our modern nations. Down through the years, progressive tax rates have traditionally sought to *redistribute* the income that corporations have so unequally *predistributed*. But, egalitarians are now asking, why give this inequality a head start? We need to do more, they argue, than redistribute income. We need to much more equally predistribute it.

The path to a "maximum wage" begins with this predistribution.

2

The Magic of Maximum Multiples

In the late 1890s, at the height of America's original Gilded Age, Bradley and Cornelia Martin shuttled between New York and London, famed for their grand bejeweled galas. In 1897, over 600 fellow fortunates attended the exceedingly wealthy couple's costume ball in Manhattan's Waldorf Hotel. A dozen guests came dressed as Marie Antoinette. Two years later, at another Waldorf affair, the lush dinner the Bradley Martins had served set the couple back $116 per plate.

At that time, laborers in New York were earning between $364 and $624 for the work of an entire year.[1]

By the early 1900s, even people of privilege were worrying about the ever-widening gap that divided the rich from the rest of society. Over the next half-century, in the United States and throughout the industrial world, people of much more modest means would mobilize to confront that gap. In nation after nation, they would struggle to redistribute the immense wealth industrial capitalism had generated.

By the mid-twentieth century, as we have seen, these struggles had left the world's industrial nations substantially – and sometimes startlingly – more equal.[2] But then, in the 1970s, the equalizing began to unravel, particularly in the English-speaking world, and levels of inequality would soon rival the Waldorf heydays of the Bradley Martins. The decades of greater equality right after World War II seem nothing more today than a cruel tease, a generation-long anomaly.

We are returning, the French economist Thomas Piketty argues, to the extravagantly unequal "patrimonial capitalism" of the early twentieth century, to a time when inheritances shape life chances far more significantly than how hard or how well people work. Piketty sees the equitable interlude of the mid-twentieth century as "a transitory period due to very exceptional circumstances," most notably the wrenching impact of two world wars and the massive subsequent reconstruction that followed. These unique circumstances have all now played out. Wealth has resumed its intense concentration.

The Magic of Maximum Multiples

Will this concentration lock us into our Gilded Age past – or worse? "Nobody knows," Piketty noted after his 2014 book, *Capital in the Twenty-First Century*, became an international bestseller. "The main message of the book is that there is no pilot in the plane. There is no natural process that guarantees that this is going to stop at an acceptable level."[3]

Stanford University historian Walter Scheidel offers an even bleaker perspective in his disquieting 2017 book, *The Great Leveler: Violence and the History of Inequality from the Stone Age to the Twenty-First Century*. Piketty sees the equality of the mid-twentieth century as an aberration, a temporary respite from the wealth-concentrating dynamics of capitalism. Scheidel sees mid-twentieth-century equality as an aberration from the basic dynamics of human society.

Inequality, Scheidel maintains, has always been humanity's default state. We only become more equal – and then only temporarily so – when "massive and violent disruptions of the established order" generate "big equalizing moments." Want more equality? Start a war, Scheidel's work suggests.[4] Unleash a plague.

The good news? Scheidel has none. On the one hand, "nobody in his or her right mind" ever welcomes violence, he notes. On the other, he sees no easy, peaceful route to more equitable distributions of income and wealth.[5]

Apologists for our unequal economic order have, predictably enough, rushed to celebrate Scheidel's thesis. His analysis, they believe, puts history on their side. Only "bloody suffering," as the Cato Institute's Ryan Bourne puts it, ever produces more equality.[6] So let's simply instead "accept the historical facts" and abandon "equality as a central ambition."

Scheidel, for his part, hasn't invited this giddy appreciation from conservatives. In *The Great Leveler*, he offers up no impassioned defense for maldistributed income and wealth. Quite the opposite. *The Great Leveler* invites us instead to think more deeply about inequality and try to come up with something "innovative and original" enough to help our societies become – and remain – more equal.

For Piketty, that something "innovative and original" would be a global wealth tax, an annual levy – set as a rate as high as 5 percent[7] – on stocks, bonds, and other assets that typically go untaxed until their owners sell them for a profit. Increasingly, these assets go untaxed even then. The world's super rich have seen to that. They've stashed a huge chunk of their wealth in opaque tax havens where tax collectors have no access.

How much wealth? The economist Gabriel Zucman, a Piketty colleague, has zeroed in on the "anomalies" of international financial record-keeping that enable tax evasion. We are living in a world, Zucman relates, where taxes on our wealthy can essentially only be collected if these wealthy "self-declare their income."[8] Ever fewer do. Zucman's virtuoso statistical sleuthing ends up concluding that the global super rich – deep pockets who hold over \$50 million in assets – had stashed \$7.6 trillion in offshore havens, about 8 percent of total global personal financial wealth as of 2014.[9]

A global tax on this enormous stash of wealth could certainly dent the grand private fortunes of the world's wealthiest and return ample new revenues to governments worldwide. But Piketty's wealth tax proposal has met with a distinct lack of enthusiasm, from both mainstream observers and even advocates for a more equal world.

"The kind of international cooperation Piketty calls for," notes the American analyst Matthew Yglesias, "is difficult to imagine happening in practice."[10]

Other egalitarians have misgivings about Piketty's global wealth tax that go beyond questions of political practicality. His wealth tax, they believe, represents just another twist on the traditional redistributive approach to curbing inequality. Let's tax our wealthiest, this approach urges, and use the revenues these taxes raise to underwrite initiatives that can help "level up" those without much wealth at all.

This redistributive approach has made an invaluable contribution. Without high taxes on the wealthy, the mid-twentieth century would have experienced no egalitarian surge. But this surge faded. The rich came back. In nation after nation, they have regained grand fortune and dismantled social advances on fronts as varied as pensions and workplace safety.

What made this political comeback possible? Critics from the left see a fatal flaw in redistribution as traditionally practiced. This redistribution has taken the inequality-generating economy as a given and essentially accepted that this economy will end up advantaging some and disadvantaging others. Egalitarians, in this perspective, have a clear role to play: They work to even up the outcomes, to smooth out the advantages.

But the advantaged seldom cooperate. They push back against the smoothing. Eventually, they break through, on tax and other fronts. Divides between the rich and everyone else once again begin to widen.

The British economist Faiza Shaheen uses a medical analogy to describe how the traditional redistributive approach typically falters. Over time, she explains, viruses can develop resistance to antiviral medications.[11] The rich, like viruses, also develop resistance, in their case to redistributive taxes. They use their wealth and power to carve out tax loopholes and lower tax rates. Their fortunes balloon. Inequality grows.

Smart public health officials stress prevention. Smart social and economic policy, says Shaheen, would stress prevention as well. This policy wouldn't solely rely on our ability to tax income and wealth that concentrate at the economic summit. This policy would instead move to prevent income and wealth from concentrating in the first place. Inequality simply matters too much to let it dig in.

We need, in short, to battle for economies that generate less inequality, not just for redistributive measures that aim to clean up the messes inequality creates. We need to place as much emphasis on the "predistribution" of wealth as its redistribution. We need to identify the economic institutions and policies that guide excessive rewards to the rich and powerful – and make them over.

This predistributive critique is resonating in the redistributionist camp. Piketty, for instance, has acknowledged that his landmark *Capital in the Twenty-First Century* may devote "too much attention to progressive capital taxation and too little attention to a number of institutional evolutions that could prove equally important."[12] Predistribution and redistribution, Piketty stresses, do not stand in opposition. Egalitarians should see them as "complementary, not substitutes."

But just how could we – how should we – "predistribute"? A number of inequality drivers, everything from intellectual property rights to land use, certainly need overhauling. But the overarching focus of the emerging predistributive thrust has been on the decades-long decline in the share of national income going to worker wages. In 2007, the US Commerce Department reported that the wage and salary share of national income had the previous year hit the lowest level since the government started tracking income shares in 1929. Corporate profits, meanwhile, had hit a record high.[13]

That trend has continued. Over the first 15 years of our new century, an Economic Policy Institute analysis details, the share of corporate income going to wages dropped 7 percentage points, the equivalent of over half a trillion dollars in lost paycheck income.[14] This declining wage share trend has been a worldwide phenomenon. Between 1990 and 2009, the OECD calculates, the labor compensation share fell in 26 of the 30 developed nations with data available. And all these numbers actually understate how much working people have lost, since the national income share numbers count both workers and executives in the labor share.[15]

This shrinking share of national income for working families makes no rational economic sense. Fewer coins in worker pockets mean either less demand for goods and services or huge increases in household debt – or both. Firms in low-wage environments, meanwhile, have little reason to invest in productivity enhancements. With so much cheap labor available to hire, why go to that trouble? Low wages also mean fewer customers who can afford to buy the goods and services that productivity enhancements would help companies produce. So companies end up awash with cash that has no place productive to go, cash that ends up fueling an endless stream of mergers and acquisitions that enhance monopoly power – and ratchet up the profit share of national income.

Our global sinking worker wage share has animated various initiatives designed to "make work pay." But corporations have shown little inclination to play along. Why should they? A low-wage economy may make no economic sense for society as a whole. But low wages make perfect sense for individual corporate executives. The smaller the worker share, the greater the corporate profit, the more generous the rewards for top corporate brass. And these rewards have no limit. The more executives exploit their workers, the more they can pocket. An ability – and willingness – to exploit becomes what makes executives attractive and valuable.

In early 2017, no executive in North America struck investors as more attractive and valuable than Hunter Harrison.[16] This veteran corporate chief demanded – and won – a $230-million four-year pay package to take the reins at the railroad powerhouse CSX. What made him worth that windfall to the CSX board of directors? Harrison, as the CEO at Canadian Pacific, had "turned around" a lackluster operation. The secret to his success? He eliminated the jobs of 17,000 Canadian Pacific employees, 34 percent of the workforce.

Cutting jobs can be strenuous work. Harrison made sure he received adequate compensation for it. During his Canadian Pacific tenure, he collected $89 million over four years, more than double the pay his CEO predecessor at Canadian Pacific had received for the same length of service.

The Magic of Maximum Multiples

Corporate boardrooms today are overflowing with executives like Hunter Harrison – and corporate directors eager to reward them. Between 1978 and 2015, the Economic Policy Institute calculates, major corporation CEO compensation "increased about 941 percent, a rise roughly 70 percent faster than stock market growth and substantially greater than the painfully slow 10.3 percent growth in a typical worker's compensation over the same period."[17]

Corporate CEOs have come to personify greed at the top. In 1965, major CEOs in the United States averaged 20 times more compensation than typical American workers. They now average over 300 times higher. Their annual jackpots have emerged as the single largest contributor to the skyrocketing income share of America's top 0.1 percent. In the quarter-century after 1979, about half the growth in that share – 44 percent – came from the compensation high-ranking corporate executives collected. Another 23 percent came from the compensation of top financial industry personnel. All told, the rewards corporate and banking power suits rake in have accounted for two-thirds of the top 0.1 percent's outrageously good income fortune.

In the United Kingdom's top 100 firms, the High Pay Centre reports, chief executives averaged 45 times more pay than workers 20 years ago. They now collect 130 times average worker pay. In the United Kingdom, the United States, and around the world, executive compensation has essentially become the locomotive of our contemporary inequality. To "predistribute" wealth more rationally, we would need to slow that engine down.[18]

Who could do that slowing? Many corporate pay reformers look to shareholders for salvation. They seek to give shareholders a "say on pay," the right to take annual votes on executive pay packages, and they also call for changes in corporate governance rules that would give dissident shareholders a better shot at unseating CEO-friendly incumbents on corporate boards.

Other reformers support these moves toward shareholder empowerment, but question the viability of any strategy that relies on shareholders – and shareholders alone – to restore common sense to executive compensation.

"Why should we let shareholders be the ultimate arbiter on the size of CEO rewards," an Institute for Policy Studies report asks, "when these rewards can and do create incentives for CEO behaviors that hurt people who aren't shareholders?"[19]

Consumers, workers, and communities all have a stake in how corporations pay CEOs. Shareholders count as just one stakeholder among many, and their interests may not necessarily align with the interests of other stakeholders.

In developed market economies, we already recognize this divergence of stakeholder interests. We do not, for instance, leave to shareholders the responsibility for making sure that corporations refrain from fouling the environment. Instead, we legislate into law rules on how corporations can behave environmentally.

By the same token, we do not expect shareholders to monitor the fairness of corporate employment practices. We deny government support, for instance, to companies that discriminate by race or gender in hiring. In the United States, such companies cannot gain government contracts. Tax dollars, Americans have come to believe, should not subsidize enterprises that increase racial or gender inequality.

Stakeholder-oriented corporate reformers are extending this analogy to executive compensation. Tax dollars, they maintain, should also not subsidize enterprises that widen *economic* inequality. Tax dollars today undeniably do. Hundreds of billions of them annually flow – as government contracts or tax breaks or outright subsidies – to companies that pay executives hundreds of times more than their workers. Executives at these companies have no incentive to change this status quo. They benefit too much from it. They win when workers lose. Their victories make inequality ever worse.

We need a new reward structure. Top executives need an incentive to share the wealth their enterprises create. A maximum wage could provide that incentive. The "public purse" could make that maximum wage practical.

Commentators tend to see economies as starkly divided constructs, the private sector on one side, the public sector on the other. But no stark divide exists in the real economic world. Public and private sectors are continually intersecting. In the United States, private-sector firms take in about $500 billion every year in federal government contracts, for everything from manufacturing military aircraft to serving food and drinks in national parks.[20] Over a fifth of the US workforce, 22 percent, labors for a company that holds one or more federal contracts. Millions of other Americans work for firms with state and local government contracts.

Governments at all levels in the United States also bestow economic development subsidies on private corporations. "Corporate welfare" from state and local governments alone totaled $110 billion in 2014, with three-quarters of that total going to fewer than 1,000 large corporations.

These subsidies do wonders for corporate bottom lines. Aircraft maker Boeing pocketed $13.2 billion in state and local subsidies in 2014, a total that exceeded the company's *total* pretax profits for the previous two years.[21]

Imagine if all this taxpayer largesse came with strings that tied top executive compensation to worker pay: no contracts, no subsidies, no tax breaks for corporations that pay their top executives – in salary, bonus, and incentives – over 25 or 50 or 100 times what their workers are making.

Such strings would be politically popular. No nation on earth has taxpayers who want to see the taxes they pay enrich the already rich. In a 2016 Reuters/Ipsos poll of over 1,000 Americans with investments in the stock market, a survey sample that tilts conservative, just under 60 percent felt CEOs at major corporations were making "too much," double the share who felt corporations had CEO pay "about right."[22] Political campaigns to deny tax support for corporate executive pay excess would find publics ready – and even eager – to listen.

And if those publics actually pressed links between corporate executive pay and government outlays into law, the consequences would be far-reaching. Corporate executives would suddenly have an incentive to *raise* long-stagnant worker wages and less of an incentive to squeeze consumers or cook the books or do any other dastardly deed that subverts the overall public well-being. What would be the point? A move to outsource jobs or cut corners on product safety still might, of course, increase corporate profits. But those higher profits would translate into executive pay windfalls only if corporations turned their back on government contracts, tax breaks, and subsidies. No major corporation could thrive without this government support. No rational corporate board would risk losing it.

A predistributive approach to public policy could also reward corporations with the most modest pay differentials between executives and workers. Governments could offer these firms lower tax rates. Or give them preferential treatment in the contract-bidding process. Steps like these would, over the long term, privilege enterprises with pay patterns that help narrow inequalities and place at a competitive disadvantage those enterprises that continue to compensate executives excessively.

The competitive *advantage*, in this environment, would go to nontraditional enterprises that embrace equity as a central core value. Cooperatives and worker-managed firms would have a better chance of prospering – and proliferating – if tax dollars no longer subsidized corporations that lavished excessive compensation on top executives. Leading egalitarian thinkers like political scientist and historian Gar Alperovitz see these alternate enterprises as the key to creating an equitable and sustainable "New Economy."[23] Placing a "maximum wage" pay ratio at the heart of the intersection between public and private sectors would give these alternate enterprises a powerful leg up – and help "level up" lowly incomes.

That same pay ratio would, over time, depress executive compensation. In 2016, CEOs at America's top corporations averaged $16.6 million, nearly 340 times the average US worker take-home.[24] Executive paychecks at that exorbitant level would start shrinking immediately if governments at all levels began rewarding enterprises that maintain a reasonable pay ratio maximum and penalizing those firms that do not.

Any paycheck erosion at the corporate executive summit would, in turn, begin deflating the income and wealth of the 1 percent. But huge concentrations of income and wealth would, to be sure, most certainly remain. If pay ratio maximums swept across the corporate landscape, already accumulated billion-dollar fortunes would continue to throw off tens and even hundreds of millions in annual investment returns. Hedge and private equity fund managers would still be wheeling and dealing their way to massive windfalls. Winner-take-all superstars in the entertainment industry would have no reason to expect or accept smaller rewards for their highly prized labor.

The super rich would remain with us in societies that leveraged the power of the public purse to cap corporate CEO compensation. But this super rich, without a steady infusion from the ranks of corporate executives, would stand more isolated and less politically potent. Their declining political influence would open the door to broader initiatives that seek to address the vast incomes that come from the ownership of assets. Societies could, for instance, begin to restructure income taxes along maximum-wage lines. Incomes above specific benchmarks – starting perhaps at 25 or 50 or 100 times the minimum wage – could be subject to strikingly higher tax rates than incomes below those ratios.

Into our sights would soon begin to creep a world without a super rich. And a dandy world that would surely be.

3

A Society without a Super Rich

Would we be traipsing on shaky social ground if we ever seriously set out to prevent people from becoming fabulously rich? Does the presence of a rich among us bring benefits no truly rational society can afford to lose? Do we need – does progress demand – grand private fortunes?

Cheerleaders for grand fortune regularly make this case. The prospect of becoming phenomenally wealthy, they avow, gives people of great talent a powerful incentive to do great things. The enormous wealth these talented accumulate, the argument continues, propels philanthropy forward and benefits individuals and institutions that need a helping hand.

Even the idle rich, as conservative patron saint Frederick Hayek once insisted, have a socially constructive role to play.[1] Wealth gives them the freedom to experiment "with new styles of living." They can pioneer new "fields of thought and opinion, of tastes and beliefs." The wealthy, in sum, enrich our culture.

The rich, these pages counter, essentially enrich only themselves. The awesomely affluent have no net redeeming social value. We could prosper, in every sense, without them. Their presence coarsens our culture, erodes our economic future, and diminishes our democracy. Any society that winks at the monstrously large fortunes that make some people decidedly more equal than others is asking for trouble.

But the trouble the rich engender often goes obscured. Most of us will spend our entire existences without ever coming into contact with anyone of enormous means. Out of sight, out of mind: In the daily rush of our complicated lives, we seldom stop to ponder how those lives could change – *would* change – without a super rich pressing down upon us.

So let's pause our daily rush. Let's ponder. An obvious initial question: Why do so many of us always seem to be rushing? Why are we stretching ourselves so thin? The answer we tell ourselves: We're doing so much, we're working so hard, to ensure our families ever more happiness.

But all our hard work, notes Cornell University economist Robert Frank, increasingly ensures nothing of the sort. Frank asks us, as an example, to contemplate the modern wedding, life's signature happy day. What Americans spend on average for weddings, he points out, has tripled over recent years.

"Nobody believes that marrying couples are happier," observes Frank, "because we spend so much more now."[2]

So why do we spend more? We spend more, the Cornell analyst notes, "because people at the top have so much more." They're spending that more on their own celebrations. Why should that matter? The rich set the consumption standard. Those just below them, the nearly rich, see the cars the rich drive and the clothes they wear – and the weddings they throw. These comparisons color what the nearly rich feel they need and unleash what Frank has labeled "expenditure cascades." People at every income level feel increasing pressure, as the rich become richer, to reach the higher consumption bar those directly above them have set.

Is this "keeping up with the Joneses" somehow hard-wired into our genes? The actual evidence points in a different direction. Genes don't matter here. How we go about distributing income and wealth does.

A Society without a Super Rich

In relatively equal nations, in societies where minor differences in income and wealth separate social classes, people typically do not obsess over "things," the baubles of modern life. Why? If nearly everyone can afford much the same things, things overall tend to lose their significance. People in more equal societies will be more likely to judge you by who you are than what you own.

The reverse, obviously, also holds true. Things become powerful markers of social status in unequal societies where most people can't afford the same things.

"As inequality worsens," in the words of Boston College sociologist Juliet Schor, "the status game tends to intensify."[3]

In markedly unequal societies, you either accumulate more and bigger things or find yourself labeled a failure. And none of us want to be seen as failures. So we do our best to keep up, by any means necessary. We go into debt. We spend what we cannot reasonably afford. The more pronounced a society's inequality, the greater the pressure we feel. Residents of highly unequal political jurisdictions, British researchers at the University of Warwick have found, will even be more likely to search online for luxury brands than residents in more equal jurisdictions.[4]

But consumption doesn't always involve deep and disturbing issues of status and power. Sometimes we buy things just because we really truly need them. But grand concentrations of private wealth, even in these situations, end up undermining the quality of our everyday transactions.

Cheerleaders for grand fortune, predictably, claim the opposite. We all benefit, they argue, when the wealthy go shopping. Bold new products, their logic goes, typically cost a pretty penny. Only wealthy consumers can afford these expensive new products. By stepping up and paying that high price, the wealthy give fresh and exciting products a foothold in the marketplace. Eventually, this "product cycle" theory holds, the prices of these wonderful new products will start falling, and everybody gets to enjoy them.

Economists who examine actual consumption patterns tell a different story. The more that wealth concentrates, Robert Frank notes in his 1999 classic *Luxury Fever*, the more retailers tend to lavish their attention – and their innovating – on the luxury market. Year by year, products come to embody ever "more costly new features." Over time, one year's high-end models become the next year's base models, as "simpler versions of products that once served perfectly well often fall by the wayside."[5]

A Society without a Super Rich

Columbia University economist Moshe Adler takes us still deeper into how concentrated wealth distorts the marketplace and leaves our lives more "dismal." Consider rock concerts. Back in 1980, the tail end of a more equal era, 73 percent of American large-venue rock concerts charged the same price for all seats. To get good seats, dedicated fans merely needed to show up early. Fast forward a generation. By 2003, only 26 percent of concerts charged the same price for all seats. And the best seats had increased the most in price.

Nothing strange, notes Adler, in any of this. In a relatively equal society, with modest differences in income between the rich and everyone else, vendors have "little to gain from selling only to the rich."[6] But that all changes when the richest among us become exceptionally rich. Vendors can charge more for what they offer – and not worry if the less affluent can't afford the freight.

The most expensive transaction most of us ever make, the purchase of a home, reflects the same pattern. The choicest homes have the best views. But only so many homes can front an ocean. People of means eager to gain these choice locations have no choice but to compete against one another. They bid up the price. The more money they have, the higher the price goes. The slightly less rich who can't afford that price then end up competing for homes with views not so quite stunning. The prices of these homes also rise. And on the cascade flows.

But the super rich don't just drive prices up. In the communities where these rich congregate, they suck the vitality out. America's "ultra-high net worth" individuals own on average nine homes *outside* the United States.[7] Most of these homes lie empty for most of the year. Their streets go lifeless. In London and other world capitals, entire well-to-do neighborhoods have become luxury ghost towns.

These ghost towns can cast long shadows. In Manhattan, developers catering to the super rich have spent recent years building incredibly tall – and thin – ultra-luxury "needle" towers. The narrowest of New York's needles, rising 77 stories, rests on a base only 60 feet wide. Why such a slender profile? Why so many floors? Developers are simply following the "logic of luxury": Our world is overflowing with super rich willing to pay a premium – up to $90 million and more – for lofty condos that take up entire floors and offer spectacular views looking in any direction.[8]

The rest of us pay a price for those views. New York's luxury towers are blocking out the sun in Central Park, Manhattan's historic commons. The shadows the towers cast, notes architectural critic

Paul Goldberger, amount to "no casual matter."[9] Someday soon, he goes on to add, Central Park is "going to look striped."

The super rich are, in effect, altering our lived environment for the worse – and not only along the canyons of New York. The lush lives these rich lead are consuming our planet's resources at a rate that's speeding the degradation of our natural world.

Between 1970 and 2000, the number of private jets worldwide multiplied by ten times over.[10] These luxury planes emit six times more carbon per passenger than normal commercial jets. Private yachts that stretch the length of football fields burn more than 200 gallons of fossil fuel per hour. In Southeast Asia, criminal gangs are supplying China's rich with illegally logged Siamese rosewood and denuding forests.[11] The top-earning 1 percent of households, one Canadian study has found, generate three times more greenhouse gas emissions than average households – and twice as much as the next 4 percent.[12]

Those rich enough to rank in the global 1 percent, Oxfam calculates, may well be stomping a carbon footprint 175 times deeper than individuals in the poorest 10 percent.[13] Still another analysis concludes that the richest 1 percent of Americans, Singaporeans, and Saudis on average emit over 200 tons of carbon dioxide per person per year, "2,000 times more than the poorest in Honduras, Rwanda, or Malawi."[14]

Our global environmental crisis would not, of course, suddenly melt away if the world's most affluent suddenly ended their profligate consumption. Our planet needs a broader, Earth-friendly institutional overhaul on everything from energy to transportation. But this fundamental overhaul will remain elusive so long as our planet hosts a super rich. These wealthy may pose our single biggest obstacle to environmental progress.

This claim might irk some admirers of Tom Steyer, the billionaire American hedge fund manager who's devoting huge chunks of his own personal fortune – and time – to the struggle for a more sustainable earth. Other men and women of immense means have also made meaningful environmental contributions, both personal and financial. They all merit plaudits. They all, unfortunately, will never be more than marginal players in ultra-rich circles. Our planet's richest simply have too much incentive to continue environmental business as usual.

That business keeps them rich. A hefty share of our wealthiest owe their fortunes to the environmentally destructive practices so common in the mining and fossil-fuel industries. In many nations, wealthy families own a wildly disproportionate share of the available arable land. Their lockgrip on this land forces poor families into habitats too fragile to safely survive farming or logging.

Great fortunes both rest on environmental degradation and blind the wealthy to it. The rich, observes the Global Sustainability Institute, have the resources to "insulate themselves from the impact of climate change."[15] Grand fortune also immunizes them from carbon and other environmental taxes that may be effective with people of modest means. The rich, the Institute notes, "can afford to pay to continue polluting."

Psychological dynamics only add to the pressure to pollute that surges through the ranks of the super rich. In their world, wealth defines personal worth. Nothing matters more than signaling that wealth with ever grander displays of what Thorstein Veblen, the most insightful economist of the original Gilded Age, labeled "conspicuous consumption." So yachts get longer, private jets go supersonic, and mansions grow relentlessly larger.

In this world of the wealthy, climate change becomes, notes journalist and activist Martin Lukacs, the "biggest opportunity yet" for the wealthy "to realize their dreams of unfettered accumulation and consumption."[16] Lukacs has been

examining Eko Atlantic, a lush, privately run arti-
ficial island now rising outside the Nigerian capital
city of Lagos. This future "Hong Kong of Africa"
bills itself as a "sustainable city, clean and energy
efficient." But that efficiency will serve only those
who can afford to live behind the island's huge
concrete walls. In Eko Atlantic, writes Lukacs, we
can see what could well become our global future:
"privatized green enclaves for the ultra rich ringed
by slums" where a "surplus population" scrambles
"for depleting resources and shelter to fend off the
coming floods and storms."

Billionaire environmentalists like Tom Steyer are,
to their credit, working to forestall this future.
But these isolated men and women of means have
nowhere near the collective resources – and political
power – of the mega rich who see environmental
activists as a threat to the corporations they run and
a personal affront to the lavish lives they lead. These
mega rich are funding anti-environment candidates,
think tanks, and bogus "grassroots" organizations.
Some even bankroll climate-change deniers.[17]

The mega rich may not prevail on the environment. Rising tides and waves of forest fires may yet
scare straight all but the most obstinate – and rich
people-beholden – of our global elected leaders. But
the mega rich are making our environmental crisis

much more difficult to confront. A world without them could be a green world. Indeed, suggests British social critic George Monbiot, only a world *without* a super rich can ever become green.

"Political systems that were supposed to represent everyone now return governments of millionaires, financed by and acting on behalf of billionaires," writes Monbiot. "To expect governments funded and appointed by this class to protect the biosphere and defend the poor is like expecting a lion to live on gazpacho."[18]

In a world of billionaires, all our problems – not just environmental degradation – become more difficult to address. Democratic political systems operate under the assumption that gathering together to collectively debate our common problems will eventually generate solutions. Unfortunately, in deeply unequal societies, this assumption does not hold. The super rich inhabit their own separate universe. They have their own problems, and the rest of us have ours. The rich have the resources to make sure their problems get addressed. Ours go begging.

Take the morning commute. The Washington, DC area, one of America's most deeply unequal metro centers, sports some of America's worst traffic congestion. No coincidence there. In starkly unequal urban regions, the wealthy bid up the price of close-in, conveniently located real estate. Rising prices force middle-class families to move farther out from job centers to find affordable housing. The farther people live from their work, the more traffic. Those American counties where commuting times have increased the most just happen to be those counties with the largest increases in inequality.[19]

How could we ease traffic congestion? We could build new roads and bridges or, better yet, extend and improve public transportation. But both these courses of action typically involve tax dollars, and the exceedingly rich usually blanch whenever someone proposes tax-funded solutions, mainly because they figure that sooner or later people will want to tax them. So officials in Greater Washington – and other unequal metro areas – have had to become creative. They've had to come up with solutions to traffic congestion that avoid any need to levy big new taxes.

Enter "Lexus lanes," segregated stretches of highway that pay for themselves by charging motorists rising tolls as traffic increases. This system works wonderfully – for motorists of means. Affluents don't particularly care how much in tolls they have to pay. They just want to get where they're going as quickly as possible. With Lexus lanes, they do. Everybody else sits and stews in traffic.

A Society without a Super Rich

Meanwhile, Washington's subway system – 117 miles of rail – has become a public embarrassment, with long delays, rising fares, and nagging safety problems. The system's chronic underfunding reflects a national trend. US investments in infrastructure have fallen off dramatically, from 3.3 percent of GDP in 1968 to 1.3 percent in 2011, a long-term decline that began at almost exactly the same time as inequality in America started rising.[20] The US states where the rich have gained the most at the expense of the middle class turn out to be the states that invest the least in infrastructure.

One explanation: Middle-class people have a vested interest in infrastructure investment. They depend on good public roads, schools, and parks. Wealthy people don't. If public services frazzle, they can opt out to private alternatives. And the more wealth concentrates, the more our political leaders tilt the wealthy's way. The wealthy do not like paying for public services they don't use. Political leaders don't make them. They cut taxes and deny public services the funds they need to thrive. And so we get more Lexus lanes that give the wealthy speedy commutes – and remind the rest of us that only the rich ever really win in societies as unequal as ours.

Would the rest of us win more often in societies

without a super rich? Be careful what you wish for, caution cheerleaders for wealth's concentration. Any society that grinds down grand fortune, they warn, would also be grinding down the billions that make philanthropy possible – and who would ever want to do that?

The celebration of philanthropy as a justification for grand private fortune began over a century ago, in an earlier unequal epoch. The celebrating continues. Philanthropy, proclaims one 2013 study from the global bank Barclays, has become "near-universal among the wealthy." Most wealthy worldwide, pronounces Barclays, share "a desire to use" their wealth for "the good of others."[21]

Headlines regularly trumpet this good at every opportunity. Bill Gates fighting neglected tropical diseases! Bono fighting poverty! Diane von Furstenberg pledging millions for parks! Publicists for our philanthropists have skillfully clouded the core charitable reality of our times: The super rich as a class don't actually give all that much – and they get back plenty from what they do give.

Our most useful – and telling – stats on the rich and their charitable giving come from the United States, the epicenter of both global grand fortune and the philanthropic impulse. At first glance, the basic giving numbers come across as profoundly impressive. In 2015, gifts of $100 million or more alone totaled over $3.3 billion.[22]

But the aura of generosity starts fading the moment we start contemplating what the super rich *could* be contributing. In 2013, for instance, America's 50 largest charitable donors gave away $7.7 billion in charitable gifts, a 4 percent increase over the year before. In that same year, the total wealth of the deep pockets on the annual *Forbes* magazine billionaires list increased 17 percent.[23]

Back in the 1990s, San Francisco money manager Claude Rosenberg, a mega millionaire in his own right, felt this lack of generosity on the part of the rich as a deep personal embarrassment. The rich, Rosenberg believed, simply didn't understand how much more they could comfortably afford to give away. If they better understood, they would surely open up their checkbooks.

Rosenberg proceeded to act upon his conviction. He funded a research group. He wrote a book and peppered the periodicals that rich people read with op-eds that detailed his basic message. His most striking point: America's fabulously rich could hike their annual contributions to charity *tenfold* and not see their household wealth plummet or even dip. In the year 2000, Rosenberg's researchers documented, households with $1 million or more in income could have given $128 billion more to charity than they actually did give and still have ended the year with a higher personal net worth than they held at the year's beginning.

Claude Rosenberg died in 2008 at age 80, his message to the super rich almost totally ignored. The vast increase in charitable giving he had hoped to inspire never materialized.[24] The reality that shames his class – that the rich contribute far less of their available resources than those with far more modest fortunes – remains philanthropy's deepest dark secret.

So the rich don't give all that much to charity. What do they get in return for what they do give? For starters, they get tax breaks. Costly ones. The general rule of thumb: For every three dollars that 1 percenters in the United States contribute, the federal government loses one dollar in lost tax revenue.[25]

America's wealthiest also get the heartfelt thanks of institutions near and dear to their hearts, most often the elite private universities they call their alma maters. In 2012, 34 of the 50 largest individual gifts to public charities went to educational institutions, "the vast majority of them," notes one analysis, institutions of higher learning "that cater to the nation's and the world's elite."[26] In that same year, not a single one of the top 50 gifts "went to a social-service organization or to a charity that principally serves the poor and the dispossessed."

The super rich have a sweet spot for cultural palaces as well. Los Angeles will soon be home to the Lucas Museum of Narrative Art, a billion-dollar edifice that will house the Hollywood memorabilia of the billionaire filmmaker behind *Star Wars*. Los Angeles already also hosts The Broad, a $140-million contemporary art museum funded by billionaire Eli Broad that opened in 2015, and the Marciano Art Foundation, a newly completed museum that billionaire retailers Paul and Maurice Marciano have installed in a grand old Masonic Temple.

Meanwhile, despite a state law that requires California's public schools to offer music, art, theater, and dance at every grade level, arts education programs in the budget-strapped public schools of Los Angeles remain woefully "inadequate," the *Los Angeles Times* reported late in 2015, with thousands of school children "not getting any arts instruction" at all.[27] Nationwide, budget cutbacks have left millions of children without art education, especially in communities of color. In 1992, just over half of African-American young adults studied art in school. By 2008, that share had dropped to just over a quarter.[28]

A Society without a Super Rich

Millions for showcasing *Star Wars* memorabilia, pennies to help poor kids create and enjoy art. Even some billionaires find these sorts of philanthropic contradictions difficult to swallow. Financial industry maverick Bill Gross sees no way "to justify the umpteenth society gala held for the benefit of a performing arts center or an art museum" when so many people around the world are suffering.

"A $30 million gift to a concert hall is not philanthropy," notes the billionaire, "it is a Napoleonic coronation."[29]

Huge gifts get the super rich these coronations – the acclaim of society – on a regular basis. Now we all, to be sure, need acclaim in our lives. We all need our egos stroked. But the acclaim heaped upon the philanthropy of the super rich helps keep our societies endangered by their predations. Give workers higher pay? Offer consumers a better deal? Be gentler on the environment? We cannot afford these indulgences, our richest tell themselves. Society values our philanthropy too much for us to rethink how we raise the geese that lay our golden eggs.

In 2005, the prestigious Memorial Sloan Kettering Cancer Center gave billionaire David Koch its Excellence in Corporate Leadership Award as a reward for his tens of millions in contributions for cancer research. These millions came at the same time Koch Industries was aggressively lobbying to stop the Environmental Protection Agency from classifying formaldehyde – a Koch Industries product – as a cancer-causing agent.

Tax deductions. Support for their pet causes. Society's gushing acclaim. What else do the super rich get from their philanthropy? They get control – over the public policy-making process. The think tanks, institutions, and organizations the wealthy underwrite shape and distort our political discourse. They define the bounds of what gets seriously discussed and what gets ignored.

The foundations our mega rich endow, notes public policy analyst Joanne Barkan, fund researchers "likely to design studies that will support their ideas." These foundations engage "existing non-profits or set up new ones to implement projects they've designed themselves." Projects in place, they then "devote substantial resources to advocacy – selling their ideas to the media, to government at every level, and to the public," even directly bankrolling "journalism and media programming."[30]

Peter Buffett understands this dynamic from the inside. He runs a foundation created by his father Warren Buffett, by some accounts America's most publicly spirited billionaire. In elite philanthropic gatherings, notes the younger Buffett, you'll see "heads of state meeting with investment managers and corporate leaders," all of them "searching for answers with their right hand to problems that others in the room have created with their left." And the answers that do eventually emerge seldom discomfort the problem-creators. These answers, Buffett charges, almost always keep "the existing structure of inequality in place."[31]

Peter Buffett dubs this comforting charade "conscience laundering." Philanthropy helps the wealthy feel less torn "about accumulating more than any one person could possibly need to live on." They "sleep better at night." Meanwhile, the global "perpetual poverty machine" rolls on – and philanthropists appear too busy patting themselves on the back to notice. Observes Buffett: "As more lives and communities are destroyed by the system that creates vast amounts of wealth for the few, the more heroic it sounds to 'give back.'"

Through all this, income and wealth distribution remains a concern that few philanthropic foundations dare to address. America's Foundation Center recorded nearly 4 million foundation grants in the decade after 2004. Only 251 of these referenced "inequality."[32]

Some philanthropic heavies, most noticeably the Ford Foundation, have of late announced a commitment to shove inequality front and center. But observers within the philanthropic industry remain skeptical about how much difference this new commitment may make. Those societies most dependent on philanthropy, notes foundation veteran Michael Edwards, remain the most unequal, and those nations – mostly in Scandinavia – that have the highest levels of equality and social well-being have the tiniest philanthropic sectors. The "small successes" that big-money US foundations have sometimes achieved, Edwards adds, "don't add up to anything that's powerful enough to halt society's slide into a permanent division between the one percent and the other 99."[33]

Generations ago, during the original Gilded Age, the millionaire soap manufacturer Joseph Fels announced to Americans of his deeply unequal time that philanthropy was only "making matters worse." Fels urged his fellow millionaires to fight for a new America that would make the super rich "such as you and myself impossible."[34]

His advice remains sound. We could survive without a super rich. Indeed we would thrive without a super rich. But could we ever actually make the existence of a super rich impossible? We turn to this question next.

4

Pipe Dream or Politically Practical Project?

The wisest among us, down through the ages, have always considered grand concentrations of private wealth at best an indulgence that no sane society should tolerate and at worst a menace to social progress and stability. And egalitarians, down through those same ages, have struggled to trim those grand concentrations. They have never – over the long haul – succeeded. The supremely rich have foiled every serious attempt to limit their excessive power and presence. Could these rich foil a maximum wage as well? Or could a maximum wage actually forge a fundamentally more equal modern society – and keep it mogul-free?

Fans of grand fortune have, of course, long considered *any* attempt to make societies fundamentally more equal a silly fool's errand. Wealth, like cream, they argue, rises to the top. Any attempt to prevent that rising – by whatever means misguided egalitarians might choose – will always only stoke envy and bring grief. And to what end? The exceptionally wealthy, goes the conservative trope, just do not have nearly enough wealth to make a real difference. A society that took all the money of the rich and spread it around would make precious little impact on the lives of average people.

"As a matter of arithmetic," University of Illinois economist Deirdre McCloskey declared in 2016, "expropriating the rich to give to the poor does not uplift the poor very much."[1]

We would all like to see life get better for modest-income households, adds JPMorgan Chase chief executive Jamie Dimon, but "you can take the compensation of every CEO in America and make it zero" and that "wouldn't put a dent" into what average families feel they need.[2]

Plutocrat-friendly politicians particularly enjoy touting what they see as the pointlessness of leveling down the exceedingly endowed. Observed US senator Lindsey Graham early in 2016: "If you took every penny of the 1 percent, including their dog, you wouldn't even begin to balance the budget."

But the actual numbers tell a different story. On Graham's claim, for instance, National Bureau of Economic Research data for 2016 show that

America's top 1 percent of households were holding over *triple* the estimated federal budget deficit *for the next decade*.[3]

Even more stunning numbers – about the growing enormity of income and wealth at today's economic summit – come from Larry Summers, the former US treasury secretary. If the distribution of income in the United States had simply remained unchanged in the decades after 1979, he notes, families in the bottom 80 percent of the distribution would each now be averaging about $11,000 more per year in income, and families in the top 1 percent about $750,000 less.[4]

These same general patterns hold true globally. In Hong Kong, real estate magnate Lee Shau Kee held a net worth of $24.1 billion in 2015, a fortune 597,000 times the city's average annual wage. If Hong Kong's 972,000 poor had an opportunity to share equally in that fortune, the *Korea Herald* calculated, each of these poor would take in $24,700. Throughout Asia, the *Korea Herald* investigators concluded, "distributing the money of the super rich" throughout their societies would be "enough to elevate" the poor into the middle class.[5]

This *Korea Herald* redistributional exercise involved *wealth*. Any sort of maximum wage approach, by contrast, would only limit the annual *income* any one individual can collect and keep. Should that distinction concern us? Wouldn't only limiting income leave those holding grand fortunes still as wealthy and powerful as ever? Wouldn't setting a maximum for *income* leave untouched the maldistribution of our world's *wealth*?

In fact, a limit on income would surely *reduce* that maldistribution.

Income and wealth do not exist in separate spheres. The one always impacts the other. A household's income, if greater than its ongoing expenses, adds to a household's wealth. And wealth, in turn, increases income. Wealth invested in bonds generates interest. Shares of stock come with dividends. Real estate brings in rent. The sale of these or any other assets can return capital gains.

But the assets the rich hold don't just generate income. They generate costs as well. Every mansion, for instance, has to be heated and cooled, manicured and maintained, guarded and insured. Multiply one luxury home by the three or five or more that many super rich own – billionaire Larry Ellison owns over two dozen[6] – and the annual outlay for upkeep can be enormous.

Other asset classes can also carry hefty maintenance costs. Jewelry, fine art, and classic cars must be suitably protected. An owner of a super yacht can expect to shell out 10 percent of the vessel's initial value in annual expenses. A typical yearly tab might include $240,000 for insurance, $350,000 for docking fees, $400,000 for fuel, $1 million for keeping the boat mechanically sound, and still another $1.4 million for the crew.[7]

For the super rich, no big deal. A billion dollars conservatively invested will return $30 million a year, nearly 10 times the annual cost of maintaining a super yacht. But what if those with the deepest pockets couldn't count on that $30 million every year? What if some variant of a "maximum wage" – a 100 percent tax levy on personal income over a set multiple of the minimum wage – limited our affluents' annual after-tax income to a mere million or two?

In that case, any super yacht would soon become a financial albatross, more pain than pleasure. Outlays for yacht maintenance would have to start coming out of a wealthy person's wealth, as would the annual cost of maintaining multiple residences – and all the other baubles the extravagant seem to feel make life worth living. The wealthy in a maximum-wage society, if they wanted to continue living life to the lavish fullest, would find themselves annually spending much more than they could pocket in income. To keep up appearances, they would have to spend down their fortunes.

Pipe Dream or Politically Practical Project?

Amid these shrinking fortunes, the pressure on the wealthy to start dumping their assorted albatrosses would soon begin to mount. Alpine getaways that go empty most of the year would become harder to justify, and the wealthy would have no good options to ease the pinch. Rent out spare extravagances? What self-respecting billionaires want strangers schlepping around in their bedrooms? Simply sell off their albatrosses? An income cap would leave the excessively endowed unable to keep the profits from any sales transactions. If the rich did go ahead and sell anyway, just to get wealth-draining albatrosses off their hands, the value of their remaining assets would plummet as the market flooded with no-longer prized luxuries.

For the rest of us, this last turn of events would be pure win-win. If billionaires en masse began to dump their excess assets, the "cascade effect" would shift into reverse. Homes and other assets would become more affordable as wealthy – and desperate – sellers scrambled to find buyers.

All these income-cap dynamics would, over time, serve to curb grand concentrations of private wealth. But couldn't we just try taxing those grand concentrations directly? We certainly could. Taxes on wealth have a long history. But direct taxes on wealth also carry some administrative baggage.

Societies that try to tax wealth must first assess

it. That can be a chore. Getting assessments right and keeping them up to date can be a tricky ordeal, especially with fine art, jewelry, and similar luxury investments. That may be one reason why the assets of the rich, outside the realm of real estate, so seldom face taxes. Another reason why only real estate faces appreciable wealth taxation: Real estate just happens to be the only asset class where the non-rich own a substantial share of the available assets. In virtually every other asset class, from yachts to stocks, the rich overwhelmingly dominate. The not-so-coincidental result: Governments typically levy wealth taxes only on that one form of wealth – real estate – that average households hold in significant quantity.

A society that successfully implemented a maximum wage would be better politically positioned to end this wealth-tax double standard. In an income-capped society, the rich could still pump money into the political process to protect their interests. But that pumping would come at a price. Outlays for political action would put the rich in the same squeeze as outlays for luxury living. These outlays would eat away at their fortunes. Massive spending on political action, under a maximum wage, would increasingly become a luxury the rich could no longer effortlessly afford.

Pipe Dream or Politically Practical Project?

Nothing about a maximum-wage approach to fighting inequality, we need to keep in mind, *excludes* the possibility of also levying wealth taxes. An income limit would steadily level down grand fortune as the cost of maintaining that fortune exceeds the annual income the wealthy can grab and keep. A wealth tax alongside an income limit – particularly a hefty tax on the wealth the wealthy leave behind at death – would speed that leveling.

Most major developed nations already do impose a levy at death on grand fortune, as either an "estate" or an "inheritance" tax, the first the term of art for a tax on the wealth a decedent leaves behind, the second a tax on the wealth an individual inherits. Both estate and inheritance taxes typically involve convoluted assessments of asset value that the wealthy can and do regularly game to minimize their tax liability.

A maximum-wage society could choose to continue and expand existing estate and inheritance taxes. Or a maximum-wage society could choose to minimize the gaming that surrounds asset assessment by only taxing wealth left behind at death when heirs turn assets they've inherited into money income.

How could this approach work? Suppose an already wealthy nephew inherits a Renoir from his dear departed wealthy uncle. The uncle's estate would pay no tax on the painting. The nephew would pay no tax on the *painting* either. But if the nephew sold the Renoir, any money he pockets from the sale would be added to his overall annual income and be subject to maximum-wage limitations. The annoyed nephew could decide to simply hang on to his inherited painting and avoid the tax. The drawback to that decision? Our poor nephew's personal fortune would shrink as he shells out cash, year after year, to insure and protect his inherited prized painting.

Our maximum-wage society, either way, would end up less unequal. Society's richest would be less rich.

Any rich facing the nephew's dilemma do have a third choice. They could choose to not stick around. They could decamp from any nation "silly enough" to impose a maximum wage and subject inheritances to it.

This threat of exit almost always surfaces whenever proposals to tax the rich start picking up steam. The notion that "tax increases aimed at the rich simply drive them away," the *New York Times* notes, has become "an article of faith among low-tax advocates."[8]

In fact, the evidence shows no significant exodus

out of jurisdictions that have raised tax rates on the wealthy. California, for instance, has had some of the highest tax rates on high-income people in the entire United States. But researchers have found more rich moving into than out of the state.

The Washington, DC-based Center on Budget and Policy Priorities has examined the major studies on taxes and migration published in peer-reviewed economic journals since 2000. "No evidence," the Center has concluded, backs up the claim "that any more than a tiny minority of people making an interstate move are deliberately 'voting with their feet' in favor of a state that levies lower taxes."[9]

The studies the Center examined did, to be sure, only look at jurisdictions that have raised taxes on the rich by relatively modest amounts. The single biggest tax increase on wealthy Californians, to give one example, came in 2013 when the tax rate on the state's top income bracket jumped from 10.3 to 13.3 percent. The wealthy might react one way if they faced a three percentage-point tax increase, an entirely different way if they faced a cap on their entire income. Any nation that dared put in place some variation of a maximum wage, defenders of privilege could argue, would surely see their wealthy flee in great numbers.

No one, of course, can say for sure exactly how

people of means might behave in the future. But we do know a good bit about their current behavior. Billionaires largely stay put, economist Tino Sanandaji found in a 2012 study for Stockholm's Research Institute of Industrial Economics.[10] Only 13 percent of billionaires reside outside the nation of their birth. By contrast, 50 percent of the world's most-cited physicists have left their birth nation. Why do the super rich stay close to home? Billionaire business tycoons, suggests Sanandaji, "know their home market best" and feel "most likely to succeed where they have an information advantage." Only a third of the billionaires who have exited their birth nations, the economist adds, have decamped to a tax haven.

New World Wealth, a South Africa-based market research firm, has analyzed the geographic mobility of people worldwide holding at least $1 million in net assets. Millionaires, this research concluded, generally migrate to take advantage of educational opportunities for their kids, to enjoy a better lifestyle, or to feel safer from crime. Some move to flee religious intolerance. In all, New World Wealth lists 11 "common reasons why millionaires leave a country" – and only one involves taxes.[11]

In a world where some nations had adopted a maximum wage, some other nations would no doubt roll out new welcome mats for would-be refugees of wealth. Welcome mats are in fact already unrolling. Since 2014, for instance, any upstanding wealthy so inclined can buy citizenship in the tiny Mediterranean island nation of Malta for just €650,000 upfront, so long as they invest another €150,000 in Maltese bonds and purchase or rent a local residence.[12] Similar offers would likely proliferate in a world where individual societies began to cap income. But several factors would work to inhibit any mass wealth exodus out of income-capping nations.

The first would be what we could call the "fixed-asset dilemma." Extremely wealthy households have millions invested in their residences, their motor cars, and other assets that do not travel abroad easily or even at all. Many wealthy leaving a nation about to cap income would move to unload assets like these. If mass numbers of wealthy made that choice, mansions and fancy cars would flood the market – that reverse cascade again – and their value would crash. Any wealthy individuals selling assets in that environment might only receive a fraction of their property's normal value. That prospect alone might persuade many wealthy to stay put.

Money in a bank, shares of stock, and other assets of a more liquid variety, on the other hand, *can* fly about from one nation to another without losing much or any value, with just a few computer keystrokes. But no keystrokes could guarantee a pain-free migration out of an income-capped nation. Consider the United States, home to more adults worth at least $50 million than the rest of the world's 20 richest nations combined.[13] The United States currently taxes the incomes of American citizens wherever they may live. Wealthy Americans who move abroad would not escape a US tax code that featured an income cap – unless they renounced their citizenship.

Would giving up citizenship end up becoming the ultimate loophole for the rich in a maximum-wage America? Not likely. The United States now levies an "exit tax" on citizenship renouncers with a net worth of over $2 million. To calculate the tax due, US officials add up the fair market value of all a renouncer's assets *worldwide* on the day before "expatriation," then subject the resulting total value to a capital gains tax due within 90 days after exiting the United States. The US tax code includes all sorts of other provisions that make life unpleasant for wealthy citizenship renouncers as well. An America with any sort of a maximum wage would no doubt maintain these unpleasantries – and even multiply them.

Pipe Dream or Politically Practical Project?

Even so, for the truly super rich, millions of dollars in tax penalties alone might not be the deciding factor in any decision on whether to migrate or whether to stay. These rich could afford most any penalty. But could they personally afford, socially and psychologically, to leave their home nation behind? Some no doubt *would* be able to exit and not look back, and these rich would find no shortage of tax havens eager to welcome them in.

Other wealthy contemplating cutting the cord might step back. In their home nations, these wealthy would have cultural connections, skyboxes at local sports arenas, and status in their communities. Many would hesitate before giving all that up. If they remained at home and faced an income cap, they would most surely be *less* wealthy than they would be if they moved. But if they did remain, they would *still* rate as among the nation's richest. If that role brings them status and satisfaction, they would still have both if they chose not to flee.

Some apologists for avarice might concede this point. Yes, they might agree, many rich would find pulling up stakes and leaving status and skyboxes behind an unsettling prospect. These rich would likely stay put – but on their own terms. If society capped the income the rich could make, this objection to limiting income goes, the rich would have no incentive to work as hard as they do. They would earn up to the cap limit, then sashay off into the sunset. They would no longer exercise their entrepreneurial imaginations. Our "job creators" would create no more. The economy would go to pieces.

A valid point? Only if you believe that we owe our employment to the richest among us. But our economies do not now revolve around or depend on the really rich, nor have they ever. Indeed, explains the eminently wealthy venture capitalist Nick Hanauer, the wealthy become really rich by creating as few jobs as they can.

"Anyone who's ever run a business knows that hiring more people is a capitalist's course of last resort," Hanauer told a US Senate economic policy hearing in 2013, "something we do if and only if increasing customer demand requires it."[14]

Rich people alone, Hanauer recounted, can never provide enough demand to keep an economy humming.

"I earn 1,000 times the median wage, but I do not buy 1,000 times as much stuff," the mega millionaire noted. "My family owns three cars, not 3,000."

Only a strong and vibrant middle class can create the demand that healthy job growth requires. The rich aren't creating this economy, Hanauer's Senate testimony added. They're killing it. A society that lets money end up "in just a few hands," he summed up, "strangles consumption and creates a death spiral of falling demand."

So if the rich and powerful aren't creating jobs, just what are they doing behind the doors of their plush executive suites? They're speeding up that death spiral. They're inventing soulless new strategies for squeezing more out of their workers. They're wheeling and dealing commodities, inflating speculative bubbles. They're turning corporate life into a never-ending jigsaw puzzle game, combining companies into monopolies that gouge consumers, then breaking the unwieldy giants they've assembled into profitable little pieces that will, in short order, become the pieces needed for assembling another monopoly. Each play in this endless game of mergers and acquisitions leaves workplaces more chaotic and enterprises less efficient.

The incentive to play this game? The key players all get to walk away with windfalls. In a maximum-wage society, this incentive would evaporate.

Apologists for our top-heavy economic order do have one thing right. The opportunity to become fabulously rich *can* be a powerful incentive. Too powerful. The hunger for ever more can become all-consuming. Those who so hunger can lose all sense of human proportion. They may shortchange their families or risk their health. At the workplace, they may lie, cheat, and steal.

A society that capped income would dull this incentive for toxic behavior. By removing the opportunity to become fabulously wealthy, a maximum wage would send throughout society a simple, ennobling message: Life can be more, life must be more, than chasing after grand fortune.

Most of us would welcome this redefinition of the good life. Most of us, after all, wake up and go to work every day without any expectation that our work will bring us fabulous fortune. We work hard anyway. We make our contribution. We don't need great wealth as an incentive. But we all *do* want to be valued for our work. In deeply unequal societies that let some keep as much as they can grab, this recognition we all crave becomes ever more elusive.

We humans value fairness. Enterprises that want all their employees to contribute their best need to value the labor of all their employees. Corporate pay patterns that reward a few at the top unimaginably more than everyone else devalue that labor, a devaluation that leaves workers disengaged. After all, if we're working at a company where top executives can make more in a morning than we can make in a year, what incentive do we have to give our all for the enterprise?

Pipe Dream or Politically Practical Project?

Corporate human resources professionals have noticed the resulting dysfunction. A 2017 business survey that quizzed over 600 HR personnel found anxiety widespread throughout America's corporate workplaces.[15]

"Employee burnout has reached epidemic proportions," concludes Charlie DeWitt, the vice president of Kronos, one of the firms conducting the survey. That burnout serves to "sap productivity and fuel absenteeism," creating "a never-ending cycle of disruption that makes it difficult to build the high-performing workforce." Larger enterprises, DeWitt's report notes, "seem to suffer more."

What's driving this burnout epidemic? Corporate human resources experts cite "unfair compensation" as the single most significant driver. The next two highest-rated drivers: "unreasonable workload" and "too much overtime/after-hours work." Who creates that excessive workload? Who demands those excessive hours? The obvious answer: the same corporate executives who benefit excessively from unfair corporate compensation systems.

Some of the world's most thoughtful business leaders understand the perverse end product that excessive rewards manufacture. Lavishly paid executives "get pulled away from their deeply held principles," notes Bill George, the former CEO of the medical technology powerhouse Medtronic and later a Harvard Business School professor. "They get seduced by money, fame, power, and glory."[16]

Executives so seduced worry constantly about jacking up their corporate share prices and making still more money – for themselves. They should be worrying instead, says George, about how to create value for customers and how to empower the employees who create that value.

Success at the enterprise level, agrees Lars Rebien Sørensen, the CEO of the Danish drugmaker Novo Nordisk, will always be "a team effort." Any reward structure that gives teamwork short-shrift will gnaw away at the internal cohesion essential to every high-performance work group.

"When we have too wide a disparity between executive compensation and workers' compensation, we create a barrier to the employee passion and engagement that all companies need to achieve their objectives," notes Sørensen, the world's top-performing chief executive in 2016, according to the *Harvard Business Review*. "If there is too big a gap between what I earn and what a blue-collar worker at my company makes, it's going to create problems."[17]

And our modern societies simply cannot afford

those problems. Our future as a human race will rest on the effectiveness and efficiency of our enterprises, on their capacity to sustainably provide products and services. To operate efficiently and effectively, our enterprises need to be able to tap into the wisdom all their employees have to offer. That won't happen so long as our economies reward the few at the expense of the many.

Some enterprises are already taking steps to create a "solidarity" environment where all employees feel rewarded – and enthusiastic about contributing to the enterprise's success. No enterprise worldwide has won more acclaim for this effort than Mondragon, a network of cooperatives named for the Basque town in northern Spain that gave it birth over 60 years ago.

Mondragon's nearly 75,000 employees work in economic sectors that range from heavy industry to retail and banking. No top executive of an enterprise in Mondragon's Spanish network makes more than six times the compensation of any employee at that enterprise. In the United States, top corporate execs can sometimes make more in an hour than their workers can make in a year. At Mondragon, no executives can make more in an hour than their workers make in a day.

How can Mondragon pay executives so little and

still find the executive "talent" necessary to run a successful modern business? Mondragon's narrow pay ratios, the cooperative's international president Josu Ugarte explains, keep hierarchies flat and information flowing freely.

"In this environment, we get all our executives from inside," continues Ugarte. "We promote from within."[18]

Efforts to force a Mondragon-style ratio mindset upon standard business enterprises, apologists for our dominant corporate order insist, could never work. Corporations that pay their executives hundreds of times more than their workers – and like things that way – could easily subvert any move to make them pay their top people no more than a modest multiple of their lowest-paid. All these corporations would need to do, the argument goes, would be to outsource their lower-paid work. That would narrow the ratio between their top executives and lowest-paid workers – and leave their executives making the same mega millions.

Could this corporate maneuver keep our filthy rich filthy? The numbers say no. Imagine we had a corporation in the United States with a CEO making $16 million a year, the current going rate for top-tier American corporate executives. Let's assume the lowest-paid workers at this corporation earned just above the federal minimum wage and took home $16,000 a year. The resulting ratio between top and bottom pay: 1,000 to 1.

Let's suppose Americans outraged by pay gaps that enormous moved through Congress legislation that levies stiff tax penalties against corporations with gaps wider than 100 to 1. What could our $16-million CEO do to avoid these penalties? Our executive could try outsourcing all the corporation's low-wage jobs. But that move wouldn't bring the company anywhere close to the 100-to-1 ratio. Getting down to 100 to 1 – without reducing CEO compensation – would require our inequality-boosting company to essentially outsource its entire blue- and white-collar workforce, everyone making under $160,000 a year.

Top executives facing a society serious about imposing limits would, in other words, have the arithmetic working against them. They would have no easy time wiggling out from under corporate pay gap limits. To believe otherwise, to believe – as defenders of $16-million CEOs would have us believe – that any move toward greater equality will always stumble in the face of "real world" avoidance strategies, reveals a mind out of touch with economic reality.

Pipe Dream or Politically Practical Project?

But can defenders of inequality make a similar claim against those of us who support limits on income? Are we totally out of touch with contemporary *political* reality? Let's see.

5

Evolving toward Equity

These pages have explored how capping the income of our richest – and linking their future prospects to the well-being of society's least favored – would enhance almost every aspect of our lives. But could we make our way politically to a society with an income maximum? Do we have a credible path that could bring us from a world where some can make more in minutes than others can earn in lifetimes to a world that respects moderation in all things, income included?

We have suggested just such a political path, a course of action that would begin at the level of the firm, the daily engine of our vast divides. Taking this path would have us working to leverage the power of the public purse against corporations that pay their executives lavishly and their workers pitifully. That leverage, we argue, could come from tying government contracts, subsidies, and tax breaks to corporate pay ratios.

Those corporations with narrow gaps between worker and executive compensation would be welcome to government contracts, subsidies, and tax breaks. Those corporations with wide gaps would not.

This leveraging of the public purse would over time reduce the enormous contribution to inequality that our corporations are currently making. But enormous inequalities, we have noted, would remain. Huge concentrations of wealth at our economic summits – our legacy of inequalities past – would still be annually generating mega billions in income.

Our egalitarian predecessors saw redistributive tax systems as the ideal antidote to unconscionably large fortunes. In nations across the developed world, they struggled for and won progressive tax rates on income and inherited wealth, and these rates helped usher in the greater equality of the mid-twentieth century. That greater equality, we have seen, could not be sustained. An approach to equity that rested on redistributing income and wealth *from* the top could not overcome, in the long term, the political power *of* the top.

The lesson for us today: We need to do more than

redistribute income and wealth that has already concentrated at the top. We need to keep income and wealth from concentrating in the first place. Successful campaigns to limit income at the corporate summit – by leveraging the power of the public purse – could move us appreciably toward that goal.

Winning a more equal "predistribution" of the wealth our corporations create would, in turn, open the political door to initiatives that take on already existing grand individual fortunes. A public that lived in a society that frowned on corporate executives making outrageously more than workers would not long tolerate *anyone* making outrageously more than anyone else. All windfalls would become suspect. In this egalitarian climate, campaigns for an overall "maximum wage" – a 100 percent tax on income above a set multiple of the existing minimum wage – could take root and flourish.

The holders of grand legacy fortunes would, of course, pull their every political string to forestall any income tax rates that reach or approach 100 percent, just as they fought and eventually defeated the top marginal tax rates of 90 percent and more that gained wide currency in the mid-twentieth century. But in societies that had won a more equal *predistribution* of wealth, these wealthy would have fewer allies and resources. Society-wide maximums would come within reach.

This political path to greater equity certainly rates, in theory at least, as plausible. But do we have any evidence that real people in real societies would ever be willing to make this path their own? Just a few years ago, we had little such evidence. We had in abundance instead isolated people of good will daydreaming about what could be.

These daydreamers sometimes sat in positions of modest influence. In St. Louis, a city at the center of America's heartland, newspaper columnist Bill McClellan asked his readers in 2006 to mull over the idea of adding a "maximum wage" to the nation's minimum. Unlimited rewards, he argued, just give top executives incentives to misbehave.

"Give us a maximum wage," McClellan urged, "and don't help a good executive go bad."[1]

That same year, Brian Iddon, a world-class chemist elected to the British Parliament, asked prime minister Tony Blair if he agreed that the salaries of those who run everything from railroads to universities had gone "out of control, especially by comparison with the pay awards being received by those who work for them." The nation, Iddon argued, needed both "a minimum wage and a maximum wage."[2]

No individual, echoed Harvard's Howard Gardner the next year in the prestigious global magazine *Foreign Policy*, should ever be taking home more than "100 times as much money as the average worker in a society earns."[3]

"Our standards of 'enough' have become irrationally greedy," observed Gardner, a globally acclaimed psychologist whose works on human intelligence appear in over two dozen languages.

Similar sentiments would sometimes percolate out from progressive think tanks. In London, the New Economics Foundation's Andrew Simms proposed a maximum wage in a 2001 address and continued advocating for a pay cap throughout the new century's first decade.[4] In November 2008, he urged the British Labour Party to "propose either a maximum wage or maximum pay ratio."[5] We desperately needed a maximum, he explained, "because highly unequal societies have a habit of falling apart."

Simms made that observation just as highly unequal societies *were* falling apart. On both sides of the Atlantic, governments were frantically working to shore up an international financial system tottering near collapse. What would soon become known as the Great Recession, the worst economic downturn since the Great Depression, was wiping out jobs and costing millions of families their homes.

This Great Recession left in its wake a much clearer understanding of the price we pay when we let income and wealth concentrate spectacularly.[6] One blue-ribbon post-mortem after another linked growing inequality directly to the Great Recession's carnage. In the United States, reports detailed how massive rewards gave power suits the incentive to engage in massive criminal activity. Financial industry executives marketed deceptive "subprime" mortgages they knew borrowers could never repay, laundered these mortgages through a corrupted financial system, and dumped the "stinking mess" – to use economist James Galbraith's apt phrase – on "American pension funds, European banks, and anyone else who took the phrase 'investment grade' at face value."[7]

In the post-crash environment, the notion that we needn't bother worrying about the rich – and how they were becoming ever richer – stood exposed as dangerous nonsense that rational societies could no longer afford to tolerate. On the streets, at august conferences, and in the corridors of legislative chambers, more voices than ever before were daring to challenge the conventional wisdom that incomes need no limits.

Evolving toward Equity

In January 2010, leading global trade union officials arrived at the annual World Economic Forum in Davos with a set of proposals that included a call for a ratio-based cap on executive pay. Philip Jennings, the general secretary of the international union body that covers service-sector workers, urged governments to "put a stop" to "the massive bonuses" the financial industry's movers and shakers had "been ripping out of the system." Limiting executive incomes to 20 times median earnings, Jennings added, "would still leave them with plenty to live on."[8]

Society routinely "gets to debate the pros and cons of the minimum wage," New Zealand political commentator Gordon Campbell mused a few months later. "Perhaps we should put as much time and energy into debating the merits of enacting a law about the maximum wage."[9]

People the world over were musing along with Campbell. In Egypt, a nation where half the population lives on under $2 a day while the wealthy luxuriate in walled compounds, income caps emerged as a prime demand of the Tahrir Square protests that toppled the Mubarak regime in February 2011. Activists marched under a slogan worker groups had been popularizing since the earliest days of Egypt's Arab Spring: "A minimum wage for those who live in cemeteries, a maximum wage for those who live in palaces."

Early in 2011, the new Egyptian Federation of Independent Unions called for a maximum set at no more than 10 times the nation's minimum wage. Egyptians, the new federation declared, have the right "to a democratic society for all, offering every single citizen a share in its wealth," a society "that does not allow the few to buy private jets while the rest of the population cannot even afford public transportation."[10]

In Spain, grassroots activists occupying public plazas in 2011 took inspiration from the beloved 94-year-old economist José Luis Sampedro, a stalwart critic of economists who "work so that the rich become richer."[11] Their protests, in turn, helped trigger an even wider surge of grassroots activism. In September, activists occupied a public square in the heart of Manhattan's Wall Street, and that action would quickly stir imaginations worldwide.

The Occupy Wall Street protests offered no single set of demands. But their shared basic message – the rich threaten our common well-being – turned the "1 percent" into a globally recognizable political shorthand. The wealth of that 1 percent, Occupiers charged with wit and verve, reflects more theft than talent. "I can't afford a lobbyist," a Chicago protester announced, "I am the 99 percent." An Occupy placard in Los Angeles: "Trickle down made us 'pee-ons.'" Another in New York: "One day the poor will have nothing left to eat but the rich."[12]

Occupy would soon fade from the front pages. But the movement's impact, mainstream observers realized, had been undeniable. "Disputes over what constitutes economic fairness," *Bloomberg Businessweek* noted, "are moving to center stage."[13] And that movement represented a colossal political shift.

Up until Occupy, calls for linking incomes at the top with incomes below had seldom advanced much beyond the political margins. Green parties around the world had regularly included maximum-wage planks in their platforms, as had left groupings like Germany's Die Linke and nationalist parties like Plaid Cymru in Wales. More mainstream politicos never ventured anywhere near that income-capping territory. But the Occupy protests, coming on the heels of the Great Recession, changed the public conversation. The wealthy now emerged as a fit topic for political debate. How the rich go about their business, mainstream elected leaders began acknowledging, needed to become the business of everyone else.

Evolving toward Equity

In the United States, one piece of legislation that emerged out of this new political environment – the 2010 Dodd–Frank Wall Street Reform and Consumer Protection Act – took a number of steps to discourage the lavish executive-pay incentives that had helped bring on the Great Recession. One step stood out and placed the United States on a practical political path to capping income. Dodd–Frank's Section 953(b) requires publicly traded corporations to annually disclose the ratio between their CEO and median worker compensation.

This particular provision drew relatively little attention in the congressional debate before Dodd–Frank's passage. Corporate lobbyists had too much else to focus on in the 2,300-page bill. But that initial corporate indifference to Dodd–Frank's pay ratio disclosure provision would turn into corporate horror after business executives suddenly realized, after the legislation's passage, all the embarrassing mischief that such disclosure could create.

Corporate America would quickly mobilize to keep the new disclosure mandate from going into actual effect. Business lobbyists besieged the Securities and Exchange Commission, the federal agency responsible for writing the regulations that would govern the mandate's enforcement. Having to calculate median worker compensation figures, lobbyists claimed, would impose a costly burden on business – and serve no purpose, one corporate-friendly SEC commissioner charged, other than "naming and shaming" CEOs.[14]

This corporate offensive – in the short term – worked. The SEC went five years without adopting the regulations needed to put the pay ratio disclosure mandate into effect. But in broader terms the corporate offensive totally backfired. In 2010, at Dodd–Frank's enactment, few Americans knew the legislation included anything about pay ratios – or even understood what pay ratios entailed. By the end of the regulation-writing struggle over Dodd–Frank's disclosure mandate, labor and public interest groups had mobilized a pay ratio mass movement. The SEC received over 280,000 comments from Americans on the agency's proposed pay ratio rule, the overwhelming majority of them in support of disclosure. The agency had never seen anything close to that massive a public response.

The Commission would go on to adopt regulations on pay ratio disclosure in August 2015. "We finally have an official yardstick for measuring CEO greed," exulted Sarah Anderson, an analyst for the Institute for Policy Studies, a progressive think tank in Washington, DC.[15]

The corporate pay ratio figures the Dodd–Frank

Act mandates will appear for the first time in 2018, and activists are already preparing to do more than "name and shame" with the results. Ratio disclosure, they point out, will narrow the pay gap between executives and workers only if corporate boards start suffering consequences for their wrong-headed compensation choices.

Progressive lawmakers in the United States are now moving to put these consequences in place. In 2014, state senators in Rhode Island passed legislation that gives corporations with narrow CEO–worker pay ratios preferential treatment in the bidding for government contracts. A revised version of that bill, introduced in 2017, sets the ratio benchmark for that preferential treatment at 25 to 1, and the new bill's co-sponsors hope to gain support from both of Rhode Island's legislative chambers. Another bill pending before Rhode Island lawmakers would impose a 10 percent "pay ratio surtax" on corporations that pay their CEOs more than 100 times what they pay their workers and a 25 percent surtax on firms that compensate CEOs at over 250 times worker pay.

"It would take an average Walmart employee 1,133 years to earn what Walmart's CEO makes in a year," noted representative Aaron Regunberg, a co-sponsor of this Rhode Island tax at the bill's introduction. "The ratio of chief executive pay compared with the earnings of median workers has increased from a multiple of 20 in 1965 to almost 300 in 2013. And it's getting worse."[16]

Similar tax legislation gained a majority in the California Senate in 2014, but not the two-thirds support needed to move tax measures into law. The co-sponsor of that Senate bill, Mark DeSaulnier, has since been elected to the US Congress, where he has co-sponsored federal legislation along the same line.

In all, five US states had legislation pending in spring 2017 that elevates corporate tax rates on companies that pay their CEOs excessively more than their workers.[17] But the first American political jurisdiction to actually enact a measure that places consequences on excessive corporate executive pay has turned out to be a municipality in the state of Oregon. In December 2016, Portland – the second largest city in America's Pacific Northwest – adopted what former World Bank economist Branko Milanovich has dubbed "the first tax that targets inequality as such."[18]

Under the new Portland statute, a company that normally pays the city $100,000 in business tax will, starting in 2018, pay $110,000 if its CEO–median worker pay ratio exceeds 100 to 1 and $125,000 if that ratio tops 250 to 1. City officials expect the new Portland pay ratio surtax to impact over 500 corporations that do business in the city. Among them, corporate giants like Oracle, Honeywell, and General Electric. In its first year, the measure will raise an estimated $3.5 million in new revenue.

The city council vote for the new Portland tax, notes Institute for Policy Studies analyst Sarah Anderson, shows "just how broad the potential political support may be for leveraging the public purse against corporate pay practices that increase inequality."[19]

The lead sponsor of the measure, local lawmaker Steve Novick, saw his tax proposal as a strike against "economically, culturally, and politically destabilizing" inequality.[20] Rising income gaps nationally, Novick noted in the tax measure's preamble, have become "a major factor in Portland's housing crisis because huge disparity in income allows high income people moving to Portland to drive housing costs out of reach of middle class Portlanders."

City Council member Amanda Fritz cited revenue as the key reason she was supporting the pay ratio measure. The millions the new tax would raise, she explained, would help fund city programs for the homeless.

Portland's mayor, Charlie Hales, based his support for the pay ratio surtax on his personal business experience at an employee-owned engineering firm. That experience, he related, had sold him on the value of narrow CEO–worker pay ratios. At his enterprise, Hales explained, "everyone worked a little harder because 'your success was my success,' and that egalitarian culture led to a strong work ethic that drove the corporation to success."[21]

The December 2016 Portland tax vote has brought the emerging new "pay ratio politics" to a much wider public, with San Francisco and other large US cities already exploring their own pay ratio options. The ranks of jurisdictions so inclined will likely expand in 2018 as headlines start greeting the first corporate pay ratio disclosures required under Dodd–Frank – unless congressional Republicans short-circuit those disclosures by making good on their threats to repeal Dodd–Frank in whole or in part.

But the new pay ratio politics appears to have enough traction to survive whatever CEO-friendly pols in Congress may throw at it. Indeed, pay ratios have now gone global. In India, the Companies Act of 2013 and the new Securities and Exchange Board of India Corporate Governance Code require firms to disclose the ratios between their top executive and median worker compensation. The first Indian ratio disclosures appeared in 2015 and revealed that top Indian execs are now making as much as 2,900 times their worker pay.[22]

In the United Kingdom, support for pay ratio disclosure extends beyond progressive circles. Late in 2016, a Conservative Party government Green Paper supported the mandatory publication of pay ratios, and several months later a House of Commons committee report on corporate governance backed the idea as well. Disclosing the ratios between top executive and worker pay, the report noted, would focus attention on those companies "that are moving in what most would see as the wrong direction."[23] In August 2017, the Conservative government announced plans to introduce new legislation that would require UK corporations "to annually publish and justify the pay ratio between CEOs and their average UK worker."[24]

The UK Labour Party has, for its part, announced plans to more actively discourage corporations that overpay their executives at worker expense. Labour will seek a "maximum income," shadow chancellor John McDonnell pledged in 2016, by capping executive pay at corporations that "undertake government work."

"We'll use public procurement to secure [narrower] pay ratios," McDonnell vowed.[25]

The Labour Party's 2017 campaign manifesto also added into the policy mix a Portland-style tax on executive excess. Under the Labour plan, a corporation that pays executives over 20 times the national living wage would pay 2.5 percent of that excess in tax. And any firm that pays over 20 times the national median wage, a higher figure, would face a 5 percent tax on the resulting excess.

No national legislature has yet placed tax or procurement proposals like these up for a vote. But society need not wait on lawmakers to get corporations to start narrowing their internal pay divides. Published corporate pay ratios can inform and inspire grassroots citizen action on a wide variety of fronts. Consumers, for instance, can organize boycotts against companies with excessive executive–worker pay gaps.

"Businesses rely on the trust of consumers," notes Wanda Wyporska, the executive director of the London-based Equality Trust. "Those companies that see executive pay rocket while the pay of their average worker stagnates will struggle to square that with discerning customers, who correctly question why some organisations see executives as talent to be nurtured, and other staff as a cost to be reduced."[26]

The politics of pay ratios offers opportunities for

meaningful grassroots involvement that no other route to a more equal world can match. With pay ratios, almost every social situation becomes a potential arena for egalitarian struggle. Students can join with university faculty and staff to demand that their institutions of higher education link top administrator salaries to a modest multiple of pay at the base. Donors to nonprofits can insist that the organizations they support limit their executive pay to a similar multiple. Workers can take pay ratio demands to the bargaining table.

Every such grassroots campaign waged would help stitch an awareness of pay ratios into the fabric of everyday life. Every victory won, no matter how small, would help people understand that the level of inequality that surrounds us has been and always will be a human construct. No force of nature leaves some of us enormously richer than others. We can choose to be more equal. Struggles around pay ratios can make these choices plain.

We can wage these struggles at every level, from local to national, calibrating each campaign to whatever political realities confront us. Lawmakers not ready to impose consequences on companies with unconscionably wide gaps? Then the fight first aims for mandatory corporate pay ratio disclosure. Private corporate power too formidable? Then the struggle starts in the public sector: No one paid with public funds should walk away with more than 10 or 25 or 50 times what any other person in the public sector makes. A 50-times ratio too politically difficult to achieve, in either a public- or private-sector struggle? Then the push becomes a call for a 100-times standard.

No magic, perfect ratio number exists, just as no magic, perfect minimum-wage level exists. Our income floors globally have evolved over time. Our income ceilings will evolve over time as well. Every ceiling we set, in whatever setting, will make society's remaining high incomes less tolerable and more vulnerable – to society-wide income-capping propositions.

These propositions have already begun percolating. In November 2013, voters in Switzerland faced a ballot measure that banned any Swiss corporate executive compensation that runs over 12-times worker pay. In effect, under this "1:12 Initiative for Fair Pay," no Swiss company would be able to pay its top executives more in a month than the company's lowest-paid workers make in a year.

Juso, the youth wing of Switzerland's Social Democratic Party, collected over 100,000 signatures to put this 12-times cap before voters. The ceiling campaign quickly won the backing of environmentalists and trade unions and displayed throughout an entertaining combination of outrage and humor. One widely circulated cap campaign poster pictured a single hamburger next to a stack of a dozen. The caption: "12 times more salary, that's enough."[27]

Corporate Switzerland – led by executives averaging 200 times worker pay – failed to see the humor. Capping executive pay, Swiss business leaders claimed, would drive Swiss companies and jobs overseas. Swiss dailies agreed with the basic business drift. None endorsed the 1:12 campaign. But the campaign remained competitive, with pre-election polls showing support as high as 44 percent. Business responded to that polling with a huge advertising blitz and ended up outspending the cap campaign by a 40-to-1 margin.[28]

Campaigners for the 1:12 cap also had to overcome the afterglow of a Swiss referendum the previous March that had successfully expanded shareholder say over executive pay decisions. That referendum, many voters apparently felt, had solved the nation's executive compensation problem.

On election day, the 1:12 cap fell by a 66–34 percent margin. Responded a disappointed Young Socialist leader David Roth: "Our opponents succeeded in making people afraid." Still, he added, an "economic system based on salaries in the millions" has "no future."[29]

Egalitarian observers outside of Switzerland agreed. The young Swiss activists, noted British social scientist Richard Wilkinson, co-author of *The Spirit Level*, had made a major contribution. They had helped the entire world understand that businesses "do not have to be organized as systems for the undemocratic concentration of wealth and power."[30]

That understanding is spreading worldwide and inching its way into our core political discourse. In the United Kingdom, polling early in 2017 found 57 percent of the British public in favor of "the government encouraging companies to introduce a cap in executive pay more than 20 times that of their lowest paid worker" and only 30 percent opposed.[31]

In the French 2017 presidential election, longshot candidate Jean-Luc Mélenchon stunned his nation's political elite with a campaign that featured a call for a cap on all personal earnings over €400,000 per year. Mélenchon pulled just under 20 percent of the first-round votes, just a few percentage points behind the leading vote-getter, Emmanuel Macron, and almost double the 11.1 percent he had pulled as a presidential candidate in 2012.

Modern societies, more and more of us are coming to see, can function with income distributions much narrower than our current distributions. Modern societies, ever more of us are understanding, can function *better* with much narrower distributions.

So are we standing on the cusp of a major maximum wage breakthrough? Not yet. The struggle for a decent minimum wage, let's remember, has taken generations – and still remains a work in progress. We won't see a maximum wage, a meaningful income ceiling set as a multiple of society's income minimum, anytime soon. But we can stride smartly toward that goal, right now, on many different fronts.

We have a path forward. We need only take it.

Notes

Introduction: Moderation in All Things, Even Income

1 Jim Davies, Rodrigo Lluberas, and Anthony Shorrocks, *Global Wealth Databook 2017* (Zurich: Credit Suisse Research Institute, 2017).

2 Larry Elliott, "Inequality gap widens as 42 people hold same wealth as 3.7bn poorest," *Guardian*, January 21, 2018.

3 Priyambada Dubey, "These filthy rich Arab kids flaunting their Rolexes, Maybachs and pet lions on Instagram will make you feel bad about your bank balance," *Daily Bhaskar*, May 4, 2017.

4 Vicki Newman, "Princesses who don't pay the bill and guests who pay £13 to have their socks laundered check into A Very British Hotel," *Daily Mirror*, March 1, 2017.

5 Rebecca Kaplan, "Obama: income inequality 'the defining challenge of our time,'" CBS News, December 4, 2013.

6 Greg Jaffe and David Nakamura, "At UN, Obama offers a defense of a liberal world order under siege," *Washington Post*, September 20, 2016.

7 Astrid Zweynert, "World's growing inequality is 'ticking time bomb' – Nobel laureate Yunus," Reuters, December 1, 2016.

8 World Economic Forum, "Deepening income inequality," November 2014. http://reports.weforum.org/outlook-global-agenda-2015/top-10-trends-of-2015/1-deepening-income-inequality/.

9 Pew Research Center, "Emerging and developing economies much more optimistic than rich countries about the future," October 9, 2014. http://www.pewglobal.org/2014/10/09/emerging-and-developing-economies-much-more-optimistic-than-rich-countries-about-the-future/.

10 ISSC, IDS, and UNESCO, *World Social Science Report 2016. Challenging Inequalities: Pathways to a Just World* (Paris: UNESCO Publishing, 2016), p. 3.

11 Maimuna Majumder, "Higher rates of hate crimes are tied to income inequality," FiveThirtyEight.com, January 23, 2017.

12 Nick Haslam, "Distress, status wars and immoral behaviour: the psychological impacts of inequality," *The Conversation*, March 26, 2017.

13 Robbie Gramer, "How does US health care stack up to the developed world?" *Foreign Policy*, March 24, 2017.

14 Lenny Bernstein, "US life expectancy will soon be on par with Mexico's and the Czech Republic's," *Washington Post*, February 21, 2017.

15 Stephen Bezruchka, "Early life or early death: support for child health lasts a lifetime," *International Journal of Child, Youth and Family Studies*, 6(2) (2015): 204–29.

16 Kate Pickett and Richard Wilkinson, "Child wellbeing and income inequality in rich societies: ecological cross sectional study," *British Medical Journal*, 335 (7629) (2007): 1080.

17 Ganesh Sitaraman, "Divided we fall," *New Republic*, April 10, 2017.

18 Sam Pizzigati, "The stealth politics of our unequal age," Inequality.org, April 2, 2015.

19 Henry Schumacher, "Inequality and corruption," *Freeman*, March 10, 2017.

20 Alexander Hijzen and Eric Gould, "Growing apart, losing trust? The impact of inequality on social capital," IMF Working Papers, August 22, 2016.

21 Andrew Berg and Jonathan Ostry, "Equality and efficiency," International Monetary Fund Finance & Development, September 2011.

22 Christine Lagarde, "The IMF at 70" (address to IMF Board of Governors, Washington, DC, October 10, 2014).

23 Larry Elliott, "Revealed: how the wealth gap holds back economic growth," *Guardian*, December 8, 2014.

24 Facundo Alvaredo, Lucas Chancel, Thomas Piketty, Emmanuel Saez, and Gabriel Zucman, "Global inequality dynamics: new findings from WID.world," NBER Working Paper 23119, 2017.

25 Cait Murphy, "Are the rich cleaning up?" *Fortune*, September 4, 2000.
26 Nina Glinski, "Blinder says wealth gap debate should focus on poor," Bloomberg, June 27, 2014.
27 Michael White, "Peter Mandelson has not lost the knack of infuriating his enemies," *Guardian*, January 26, 2012.
28 Alvaredo et al., "Global inequality dynamics."
29 World Bank, *Poverty and Shared Prosperity 2016: Taking on Inequality* (Washington, DC: World Bank, 2016).
30 Neil Gough, "Hong Kong wealth gap on display in protests," *New York Times*, October 5, 2014.
31 Dan Bloom, "Hong Kong's 'caged dogs,'" *Daily Mail*, February 13, 2014.
32 Peter Edelman, *So Rich, So Poor: Why It's So Hard to End Poverty in America* (New York: New Press, 2013).

Chapter 1 Defining Excess

1 Felix Adler, "Social reform: proposing a system of grand taxation," *New York Times*, February 9, 1880.
2 Emmanuel Saez and Thomas Piketty, "Income inequality in the United States, 1913–1998," *Quarterly Journal of Economics*, 118(1) (2003). (Tables and figures updated to 2015, June 2016.) https://eml.berkeley.edu/~saez/TabFig2015prel.xls.
3 The World Wealth and Income Database offers the most comprehensive comparative distributional statistics.

4 Duncan Norton-Taylor, "How top executives live," *Fortune*, 1955. Reprinted in *Fortune*, May 6, 2012.

5 Ian Ayres and Aaron Edlin, "Don't tax the rich. Tax inequality itself," *New York Times*, December 18, 2011.

6 Jan Pen, *Income Distribution: Facts, Theories, Policies* (New York: Praeger, 1971).

7 Henry Phelps Brown, *Egalitarianism and the Generation of Inequality* (Oxford: Clarendon Press, 1988), p. 466.

8 Herbert Inhaber and Sidney Carroll, *How Rich Is Too Rich? Income and Wealth in America* (New York: Praeger, 1992).

9 Saez and Piketty, "Income Inequality in the United States, 1913–1998."

Chapter 2 *The Magic of Maximum Multiples*

1 Michael McGerr, *A Fierce Discontent: The Rise and Fall of the Progressive Movement in America, 1870–1920* (New York: Free Press, 2003), pp. 4–16.

2 World Wealth and Income Database, http://wid.world/.

3 Bernard Condon, Josh Boak, and Christopher Rugaber, "Q&A: a French economist's grim view of wealth gap," Associated Press, April 23, 2014.

4 Elena Dancu, "Historian uncovers a grim correlation between violence and inequality over the millennia," Phys.Org, January 24, 2017.

5 Walter Scheidel, *The Great Leveler: Violence and the History of Inequality from the Stone Age to*

the Twenty-First Century (Princeton: Princeton University Press, 2017), p. 436.

6 Ryan Bourne, "Want a more equal society? Be careful what you wish for," *City A.M.*, February 14, 2017.

7 Thomas Piketty, *Capital in the Twenty-First Century* (Cambridge, MA: Belknap Press, 2014). See Ch. 15 and Ch. 12, Tables 12.1–12.2.

8 Gabriel Zucman, "The missing wealth of nations: are Europe and the US net debtors or net creditors?" *Quarterly Journal of Economics*, 128(3) (2013): 1321, 1327.

9 Matt Phillips, "Secret bank accounts, income inequality – and why Luxembourg matters," *Quartz,* October 1, 2015.

10 Matthew Yglesias, "The short guide to *Capital in the Twenty-First Century*," *Vox*, April 8, 2014.

11 Cited in Sam Pizzigati, "Why greater equality strengthens society," *Nation*, December 6, 2011.

12 Thomas Piketty, "Capital, predistribution and redistribution," *Crooked Timber*, January 4, 2016.

13 Isaac Shapiro and Aviva Aron-Dine, "Share of national income going to wages and salaries at record low in 2006," Center for Budget and Policy Priorities, March 29, 2007.

14 Josh Bivens, "The decline in labor's share of corporate income since 2000 means $535 billion less for workers," Economic Policy Institute, September 10, 2015.

15 Timothy Taylor, "Labor's falling share, everywhere," *Conversable Economist*, June 6, 2013.

16 Frederic Tomesco, "CSX bets more than $200 mil-

lion Harrison can spur turnaround," Bloomberg, March 7, 2017.

17 Lawrence Mishel and Jessica Schieder, "Stock market headwinds meant less generous year for some CEOs," Economic Policy Institute, July 12, 2016.

18 Polly Toynbee, "Theresa May promised to tackle greedy bosses – instead she's helping them," *Guardian*, May 2, 2017.

19 Institute for Policy Studies and United for a Fair Economy, *Executive Excess 2006* (Washington, DC: Institute for Policy Studies, 2006), p. 41.

20 "Breach of contract: how federal contractors fail American workers on the taxpayer's dime," Office of Sen. Elizabeth Warren, US Senate, 2017.

21 Phil Mattera, "Subsidizing the corporate one percent," Good Jobs First, February 25, 2014.

22 "Investors want their money managers to challenge CEO mega salaries," Reuters, April 27, 2016.

23 "The cooperative economy: a conversation with Gar Alperovitz," *Orion*, June 5, 2014.

24 Kari Paul, "Salaries for employees were stagnant last year as CEOs got even richer," *MarketWatch*, April 13, 2017.

Chapter 3 A Society without a Super Rich

1 George Monbiot, "Neoliberalism: the deep story that lies beneath Donald Trump's triumph," *Guardian*, November 14, 2016.

2 Sam Pizzigati, "Our grand fortunes, our grand waste," Inequality.org, February 8, 2015.

3 "The overspent American: an interview with Juliet Schor," *Multinational Monitor*, September 1998.

4 Peter Ubel, "How the psychology of income inequality benefits luxury brands," *Forbes*, February 28, 2017.

5 Robert Frank, *Luxury Fever* (New York: Free Press, 1999), pp. 25, 11.

6 Moshe Adler, *Economics for the Rest of Us: Debunking the Science That Makes Life Dismal* (New York: New Press, 2011), p. 76.

7 Lucinda Shen, "Here's how many homes the average billionaire now owns," *Fortune*, December 2, 2016.

8 "Sky high: the logic of luxury," a Skyscraper Museum exhibition (New York, October 9, 2013 through June 15, 2014).

9 Paul Goldberger, "Too rich, too thin, too tall?" *Vanity Fair*, April 9, 2014.

10 Chuck Collins, John Cavanagh, Robert Weissman, Sam Bollier, and Sarah Anderson, *High Flyers: How Private Jet Travel is Straining the System, Warming the Planet, and Costing You Money* (Washington, DC: Institute for Policy Studies, 2008).

11 Environmental Investigation Agency, *Routes of Extinction: The Corruption and Violence Destroying Siamese Rosewood in the Mekong* (London: Environmental Investigation Agency, 2014).

12 Robert Frank, "Hybrid-powered megayachts come with green bragging rights," *New York Times*, August 22, 2015.

13 Timothy Gore, "Extreme carbon inequality," Oxfam International, December 2, 2015.

14 Lucas Chancel and Thomas Piketty, *Carbon and Inequality: From Kyoto to Paris* (Paris: Paris School of Economics, 2015).

15 Dario Kenner, "The inequality of overconsumption: the ecological footprint of the richest," Global Sustainability Institute Working Paper No. 2015/2, November 2015.

16 Martin Lukacs, "New, privatized African city heralds climate apartheid," *Guardian*, January 21, 2014.

17 Andy Rowell, "The reclusive climate denying puppetmaster behind Trump," Oil Change International, March 20, 2017.

18 George Monbiot, "The earth cannot be saved by hope and billionaires," *Guardian*, June 19, 2012.

19 Robert Frank, "Income inequality: too big to ignore," *New York Times*, October 18, 2010.

20 David Madland and Nick Bunker, "Ties that bind: how a strong middle class supports strong public infrastructure," Center for American Progress Action Fund, March 22, 2012.

21 "Origins and legacy: the changing order of wealth creation," Barclays Wealth Insights, Vol. 17 (2013).

22 Chuck Collins, Helen Flannery, and Josh Hoxie, *Gilded Giving: Top-Heavy Philanthropy in an Age of Extreme Inequality* (Washington, DC: Institute for Policy Studies, 2016).

23 Aimee Picchi, "How the super-rich are skimping on charitable gifts," CBS News, February 14, 2014.

24 Dennis Hevesi, "Claude Rosenberg, advocate for philanthropy, is dead at 80," *New York Times*, May 8, 2008.

25 Stephanie Strom, "Big gifts, tax breaks and a debate on charity," *New York Times*, September 6, 2007.

26 Ken Stern, "Why the rich don't give to charity," *Atlantic*, April 2013.

27 Zahira Torres and Ryan Menezes, "Only 35 LA public schools get an A in supporting the arts," *Los Angeles Times*, November 2, 2015.

28 Valeriya Metla, "School art programs: should they be saved?" *Law Street*, May 14, 2015.

29 Strom, "Big Gifts, Tax Breaks and a Debate on Charity."

30 Joanne Barkan, "Plutocrats at work: how big philanthropy undermines democracy," *Dissent*, Fall 2013.

31 Peter Buffett, "The charitable-industrial complex," *New York Times*, July 26, 2013.

32 Benjamin Soskis, "Can funds started by the rich really stomp out inequality?" *Chronicle of Philanthropy*, August 3, 2015

33 Michael Edwards, "The privilege of being privileged," *Transformation*, October 17, 2016.

34 Benjamin Soskis, "Parks and accumulation," *New Yorker*, November 21, 2013.

Chapter 4 Pipe Dream or Politically Practical Project?

1 Deirdre McCloskey, "Growth, not forced equality, saves the poor," *New York Times*, December 23, 2016.

2 Claire Boston and Hugh Son, "Dimon says iPhones, cars help balance out US income inequality," Bloomberg, September 17, 2015.

3 Clay Wirestone, "Lindsey Graham says taking 'every penny' from wealthiest 1 percent won't balance budget," Politifact New Hampshire, March 27, 2015.

4 Lawrence Summers, "It can be morning again for the world's middle class," *Financial Times*, January 18, 2015.

5 Hong Seung-wan, Cheon Ye-seon, Bae Ji-sook, Yoon Hyun-jong, Min Sang-seek, Kim Hyun-il, and Sang Youn-joo, "What if the superrich gave their wealth to the poor?" *Korea Herald*, November 3, 2015.

6 "The incredible real estate portfolio of Oracle billionaire Larry Ellison," *Business Insider*, April 26, 2015.

7 Michael Gadd, "$400,000 in fuel, $350,000 for docking and $1.4m in wages," *Daily Mail*, January 31, 2015.

8 James Stewart, "The myth of the rich who flee from taxes," *New York Times*, February 15, 2013.

9 Michael Mazerov, "State taxes have a negligible impact on Americans' interstate moves," Center on Budget and Policy Priorities, May 8, 2014.

10 Tino Sanandaji, "The international mobility of the super-rich," Research Institute of Industrial Economics, February 14, 2012.

11 *The 2017 Global Wealth Migration Review* (Johannesburg: New World Wealth, 2017).

12 Max Holleran, "For the wealthy, citizenship at a premium," *Boston Review*, October 11, 2016.

13 Davies et al., *Credit Suisse Global Wealth Databook 2016*.

14 Nick Hanauer, Testimony before the Subcommittee on Economic Policy, US Senate Committee on Banking, House, and Urban Affairs, June 5, 2013.

15 "The employee burnout crisis: study reveals big workplace challenge in 2017," *Workplace Trends*, January 9, 2017.

16 Alexis Terrell, "Are CEOs ruining America? How bigger paychecks translate into poor leadership," Vail Trail, July 2, 2007.

17 Adi Ignatius, "What CEOs really worry about," *Harvard Business Review*, November 2016.

18 Sam Pizzigati, "A company that manufactures equality," Inequality.org, June 2, 2015.

Chapter 5 Evolving toward Equity

1 Bill McClellan, "Give executives a break – stop foisting all that money on them," *St. Louis Post-Dispatch*, March 17, 2006.

2 Gareth Tidman, "Put limit on soccer salaries – Iddon," *This Is Lancashire*, May 31, 2006.

3 Howard Gardner, "Inequality," *Foreign Policy*, May/June 2007.

4 Andrew Simms, "We should introduce a maximum wage," *Independent*, June 19, 2001.

5 Andrew Simms, "How Labour could fix the financial system," *Guardian*, November 5, 2008.

6 Matthew Drennan, *Income Inequality: Why It Matters and Why Most Economists Didn't Notice* (New Haven: Yale University Press, 2015).

7 James Galbraith, "Tremble, banks, tremble," *New Republic*, July 9, 2010.

8 International Trade Union Confederation, "Davos: corporate greed has to stop," ITUC OnLine, January 26, 2010.

9 Gordon Campbell, "New Zealand: what about a maximum wage?" *Wellingtonian*, March 11, 2010.

10 Sam Pizzigati, "Here's what democracy, economically, looks like," *Too Much*, June 30, 2011.

11 "Spanish author José Luis Sampedro dies at 96," Agence-France Presse, April 10, 2013.

12 Sam Pizzigati, "OWS revives the struggle for economic equality," *Nation*, October 26, 2011.

13 David Lynch, "Growing income gap may leave US more vulnerable to crisis," *Bloomberg Businessweek*, October 13, 2011.

14 Marcy Gordon, "SEC requires companies to reveal CEO-vs-worker pay gap," *Inc*, August 6, 2015.

15 Marcy Gordon, "Under new SEC rule, companies will have to reveal pay gap between CEOs and employees," *US News & World Report*, August 5, 2015.

16 "Regunberg introduces bill to charge surtax to companies with high CEO-to-median-worker pay ratios," *State of Rhode Island General Assembly News*, January 18, 2017.

17 Sharon Lee, "Income inequality battle brewing at state-level," BNA, March 1, 2017.

18 Nicky Woolf, "Portland to vote on taxing companies if CEO earns 100 times more than staff," *Guardian*, December 5, 2016.

19 Sarah Anderson, "This city just came up with a novel way to fight inequality," *Nation*, December 8, 2016.

20 Steve Novick, "Obscene pay inequality bad for workers and economy," *Oregonian*, December 14, 2016.

21 Anderson, "This city just came up with a novel way to fight inequality."

22 "Runaway pay," *Hindu*, July 8, 2015.

23 "Corporate governance," House of Commons Business, Energy and Industrial Strategy Committee, Third Report of Session 2016–17, April 5, 2017.

24 "World-leading package of corporate governance reforms announced to increase boardroom accountability and enhance trust in business," Department for Business, Energy & Industrial Strategy, August 29, 2017.

25 May Bulman, "Labour to set a 'cap' on salaries of top executives in Government-employed companies," says John McDonnell, *Independent*, April 19, 2017.

26 Wanda Wyporska, "Mind the gap: how pay ratio reporting can help reduce inequality," Open Democracy, December 5, 2016.

27 "Swiss vote against cap on executive pay," AFP, November 25, 2013.

28 John Lichfield, "Swiss voters reject '1:12' proposal to cap top executives' pay in latest referendum," *Independent*, November 24, 2013.

29 "Swiss reject '1:12 initiative' on pay," Associated Press, November 24, 2013.

30 Sam Pizzigati, "A daring Swiss bid to stomp out CEO

pay excess," Bill Moyers & Company, November 19, 2013.

31 Ashley Cowburn, "Majority of public support Jeremy Corbyn's plans to cap bosses' salaries, poll suggests," *Independent*, January 14, 2017.